Rasika—
Thanks for
your leadership!
B Morse

You Got This:
How to Make Big Decisions at Small Hospitals

A Novel

Doug Morse, MBA, MA

DMorseSolutions, LLC
Des Moines, Iowa

For rights and permissions, please contact:
Doug Morse
505 5th Avenue
Des Moines, Iowa 50309
doug.morse@exechq.com

Foreword published by arrangement with the author

ISBN: 979-8-218-10648-5 (paperback)

Printed in the United States of America
Cover Design by Lauren Dettmer

CONTENTS

FOREWORD

I was a new Chief Medical Officer - Senior Vice President of Physician Integration when I met Doug Morse. As a physician relatively new in a leadership role, I believed it was expected that I know the answers and have an opinion on any decision made. I was accustomed to people asking me the questions and me giving the answer. That is why I went to school and residency for eleven years – to be the expert.

Two weeks into my new role, the administrative team had a very tense and non-productive meeting about a significant hospital decision. As the meeting ended, Doug invited me to lunch. For forty minutes he just listened to me rant. He then asked a few questions, yet offered no advice. This was the beginning of our friendship and the real beginning of my leadership journey - one I am still on today.

You Got This: How to Make Big Decisions at Small Hospitals is an artful and entertaining story which assists you on your own leadership journey. Through the main character, rural hospital CEO Jack McGee, we see an individual struggle with self-doubt and a strong desire to solve problems on his own. We feel Jack's frustration until he begins to realize the power is in the question, not the answer. The clever plot helps you understand the details of a Five Step mission discernment journey while at the same time making you care for and root for the entire community as they struggle through this tough decision.

Reading this novel was energizing and created a spirit of the possible.

This is a different leadership self-help book, written as a novel, because it intertwines a singular realistic event into an intriguing journey of mission discernment and personal discovery. The process outlined has practical application for decision-making that can be applied to a wide variety of situations. Anyone involved in creating consensus, leading others, discernment, or who is part of a community – essentially all of us – can benefit from the lessons learned in this story.

This adventure reminds us to return to our personal and organizational values to make tough decisions and bring people together.

Follow the teachings here, and hopefully, like Jack McGee, you too will be "wired, not tired" as you feel the possibilities of more perspectives and new ideas to tackle tough problems.

Paul Manternach, M.D.

PROLOGUE
CEO Evaluation Discussion

"Everything was a damn mess, plain and simple," Merrill Stricker said. "There's no other way to say it, Jack."

Jack McGee just stared down at the table.

Merrill continued, "Anxious Board members. Unhappy doctors. Angry staff. Upset community. When it all started twelve months ago, I received more negative phone calls and grocery store questions than my other seven years on the Board combined."

Long pause, and then Merrill broke into a smile. "I'm pleased to say the situation today is a much different story."

Even with the kind words, Jack felt jittery. Rural hospital CEO evaluation conversations always created a bit of tension, even when everyone knew each other well.

At thirty years old, Jack had been CEO at the hospital for a little less than eighteen months. His first CEO role had been leading a critical access hospital in a smaller community in a neighboring state. With a community population of just 1,600, Jack had led that small facility for two years before taking his current position. Prior to that, Jack had been Special Projects Director for a large rural hospital system. He and his wife Amy had met in college and then married while Jack was in graduate school earning a master's degree in healthcare administration.

A stay-at-home mom with an elementary education degree, Amy took care of the couple's three-year old son, Charlie. The couple had not yet told anyone that they were expecting their second child. Jack didn't want to, as he called it, "officially" share the news yet. That's just the way Jack is, Amy had told her mother in private.

There was an air of formality as the four meeting participants sat in swivel chairs around the large wooden conference room table in the hospital Board Room.

As the dean of the local community college just a few years from retirement, Merrill was a seasoned hospital and community advocate. He had served as the Chair of the hospital Board of Trustees long enough to have seen everything, at least until this past year.

As Merrill adjusted his reader glasses, Board Member Janice Holden sat beside him holding a newspaper clipping. Janice had recently retired after many years as a local real estate agent.

Shawn Deringer, a representative from a partner health system, opened his leather binder and sat with his legs comfortably crossed and hands folded, patiently waiting. With over fifteen years experience supporting rural hospitals, Shawn had participated in many CEO evaluation conversations. Few, however, reflected a year like the one they had just experienced.

Merrill paused to glance through his papers. "You saw the positive provider comments in the written part of your evaluation, didn't you?" he asked Jack. "Eight providers completed the input forms and hardly a negative word."

"I noticed," Jack replied. "That was really nice to see, especially compared to where we were a while ago."

"I had dinner and a long conversation with the hospital's largest donor last week," Merrell said. "We all know how concerned he was, early on. He and his family are extremely pleased with how things are going now."

Merrill continued, "Just this morning a young mother stopped me while I was walking into the hospital," Merrill said. "She was holding her newborn baby and wanted the Board to know how much she appreciated being able to come here when she was pregnant, and then again after she had the baby."

Janice smiled and held a clipping from the local newspaper in her hands. "The positive newspaper editorial this week really said it well."

"*We can look back now and agree difficult decisions were necessary to maintain the hospital*," Janice read. "*The Board and administrative team made changes quickly with unparalleled transparency and recognized that local collaboration is the key to any small-town success.*"

Merrill addressed Jack again. "After a rough start, you led us on a journey that was not easy or popular at the time," he said. "But we can look back now and agree we took the right steps, the right way, for the best result."

Jack nodded with a small, satisfied smile.

Shawn offered a summary. "Let's see: positive provider comments about the CEO, improved financial results, favorable editorials and people stopping Board members in parking lots with compliments," he said. "Safe to say the situation is so much better today."

Looking at Jack, he asked, "Does it feel like it has been a whole year since it started?"

It seems like just yesterday and ten years ago at the same time, Jack thought to himself.

Chapter 1

Dr. Powerful Visiting Specialist

"**EHHHHRIIIIINNNGG!!**" the fire alarms screamed. Even though Jack knew a fire drill was due that afternoon, he still startled as much as everyone else.

A sunny, warm afternoon, four or five hospital employees had gathered for an afternoon soda in the bright, spacious rural hospital cafeteria. Jack made it a point at least once each day to spend time there. Breakfast, midmorning, lunch, evening, no matter the time, that space was the gathering spot for employees to eat, have a laugh or catch someone about a quick work matter.

The conversation had been mostly one employee's update about her trip yesterday to take her husband to a medical appointment some forty-five miles away at a larger referral hospital. The long day had ended by squeezing in a stop at Costco while her husband waited in the car. Combining doctor visits with stops at big box stores was a fact of rural life because some items just are not available locally in a town of 3,100 residents.

"Thank goodness I have a job and my insurance is good," she had said to the cafeteria group, glancing at Jack. "Otherwise we would be falling apart."

Jack felt the pang of responsibility. *The stakes are real every day,* he thought to himself.

But nothing held together in that moment because the fire alarms were blaring. Not just loud. They were LOUD. REALLY LOUD. Blaring. Blasting. Painful.

"*What on earth*?" Jack thought as he left the cafeteria to find Rich Stevens, the veteran maintenance leader. Rich knew every inch of the building and offered round the clock dedication to keep things functioning.

Jack had spent time in many rural facilities over his healthcare administration career.

Never had he heard fire alarms so obnoxiously loud.

Jack started his search for Rich in the main patient waiting lobby. A boy about 9 years old had his fingers in both ears and looked like he wanted to cry. An elderly woman cupped her hands over both sides of her head. A man in bib overalls simply hobbled toward the front door shaking his head in disgust. Various employees stood shaking their heads looking very, very annoyed.

A teenage girl sat in her lobby waiting room chair staring at her phone, oblivious to it all.

With fire alarms still **SCREAMING**, Jack took a hard right through the lobby and quickly swiped his name badge to enter the secure obstetrics unit. He thought he had seen Rich through the thin glass windows on the unit door.

Renovated just two years ago, before Jack's arrival, this particular project had been the talk of the town. Generous donors had made sure this obstetrics unit rivaled much larger institutions in every way.

The unit was empty at the moment and most lights were off. Jack strode past gorgeous artwork on the walls and glanced into beautiful, shining obstetrics patient rooms which function as labor, delivery, recovery and postpartum rooms. Brand new patient beds were perfectly made and the equipment was in pristine condition. The hallway smelled clean and looked meticulously tended.

"Delivering babies says everything about our community," a local community leader had explained to Jack during his interview process. "When babies are born in town, they stay and grow up here. That's how the town grows."

At the time, Jack had simply nodded.

Still looking for Rich, Jack walked so quickly that he was getting short of breath. Finally Jack saw Rich down the surgery hallway and gave him one of those palm-lift, shoulder-shrugs-with-puzzled-look gestures to communicate "what the hell?" as Jack strode up to him.

Rich had a wide grin on his face.

"TURN DOWN THE VOLUME ON THOSE ALARMS!" Jack yelled.

"THEY'LL GO OFF IN A FEW SECONDS!" Rich yelled back.

Jack wondered if deep down Rich was enjoying the spectacle and the reaction.

As promised, a few seconds later the alarms stopped.

Ears now ringing, Jack asked "Why are those alarms so loud?"

"That's the volume required by the Fire Marshall," Rich replied.

"I doubt that," Jack said. "Other facilities pass the inspection with alarms at a much lower volume. The patients and everyone else looked miserable."

"I don't want the Fire Marshall to write me up," Rich replied.

Jack paused, knowing this moment would be an opportunity to demonstrate his patience, his willingness to explore alternatives and his ability to quietly listen to different perspectives and communicate with caring candor.

"Please just turn them down," he said and walked away.

Jack could see clinic employee Janet Herzinger hustling toward him down the hallway, looking relieved that she had found him.

Something's up, Jack thought.

An upbeat, capable nurse, Janet had worked at the organization for five years.

"Dr. Powerful Visiting Specialist is upset about the fire alarms and wants to see you *right now,*" she said.

Like other critical access hospitals, the facility had a Specialty Clinic area where visiting medical specialists saw local patients. Visiting specialist providers arrive on a monthly schedule and spend a few hours at the facility seeing patients. These providers are very important to rural hospitals because patients get quality specialty care and the provider orders ancillary tests and/or performs procedures locally.

To the CEO and Board members, "orders ancillary tests and/or performs procedures locally" means revenue. One specialist can represent large amounts of money needed for the hospital to pay employee salaries, buy equipment and cover other escalating expenses.

Because some small rural hospitals may have only a handful of visiting specialists on a rotating monthly basis, if a provider cancels for some reason, patient care is disrupted and the hospital later sees the revenue drop for that month in the financial statements.

Of course this is the day Dr. Powerful is on-site, Jack thought as he hustled to the specialty clinic area.

It was obvious Dr. Powerful was very angry when Jack opened the door and entered the specialty clinic hallway. It was unusually quiet and several employees were looking wide-eyed, directly at Jack.

Thankfully, patient exam rooms were empty as the clinic was finished seeing patients for that day.

Dr. Powerful saw Jack and said, "This is RIDICULOUS! Those alarms are too loud! I've been in hospitals across this country and have never heard anything at that volume! I should report this facility to OSHA. I'm not coming here anymore if this is how you treat patients, and…"

Jack leaned forward and cupped his hand over his ear and interrupted him. "What?" Jack said loudly.

The doctor stopped and gave Jack a puzzled look.

Jack kept his hand cupped over his ear. Still speaking loudly, Jack said, "Sorry Doctor. I can't hear you. And I can't hear you because those alarms were so loud I think I just lost my hearing."

Brief pause. Then Dr. Powerful burst out laughing.

Janet and the staff in the room exhaled and laughed and shot relieved glances at one another.

"Doctor, those fire alarms are insanely loud and I promise they will be turned down as much as possible before the sun sets today," Jack continued. "You won't have this problem again when you come to our facility."

Whether he believed Jack or not, Dr. Powerful chuckled and started to pack his bag to leave. "Sounds good," he said.

Fortunately, the popular physician was still grinning and shaking his head as he made his way toward the exit. Apparently he would be coming back.

Jack stood with the team as they all watched the door close. Collective sigh of relief.

"Thank you," Janet said to Jack.

"Heavens, no, thank you all," Jack replied. "You do a great job serving patients and keeping providers satisfied. Not an easy task."

"Dr. Powerful seemed pleased when he left," Janet said. "Good thing, because around here, when it comes to providers and key clinical staff, we don't have a person to spare."

Chapter 2

Like a Flower and a Bee

Jack leaned over the handlebars and easily coasted past the library and City Hall. Just three blocks long, this particular section of Main Street had a slight downhill slope which made it easy to gently pedal or coast his twenty-speed bicycle past the various storefronts.

Jack glided past an auto body shop playing its radio loud enough to hear the hospital marketing director's upbeat voice finish an advertisement with the hospital's current "*Community is our Middle Name*" marketing campaign. Jack made a mental note to compliment the leader on the piece.

Riding his bicycle was a favorite perk of small town living. During most months, Jack could ride the five minute commute wearing a buttoned collared shirt and tie with dress slacks and a small backpack over his shoulder. He would arrive at the office energized from the exercise, but not too harried to need a change of clothes.

As he rode along the main street enjoying the bright sunshine and moderate temperature, Jack noticed nearly every storefront space was occupied. Women's clothing shop. Insurance office. Bar. Nail salon. Bank. Pizza and chicken restaurant. Dinner cafe. Karate studio. Most shops were closed at this early hour, although the parked cars and people coming and going made it obvious the coffee shop was alive and well at 7:15 am.

Jack took a mental roll call as he slowly rode past the glass storefronts. Women's clothing store? Husband worked at the hospital. Insurance office? Wife worked at the clinic. Bar? Owner's wife worked at the hospital. Nail salon? Owner worked part-time at the hospital. Bank? Probably twenty or so bank employees had spouses, siblings or parents who worked at the hospital. Karate studio? One of the clinic physicians was a second-degree Blackbelt and started the club to teach classes several times per week.

"Good morning, Jack!" the local financial representative said as he exited the coffee shop with latte in hand. "Have a good one!"

Jack nodded with a wide smile while holding onto the handlebars.

"You, too!" he yelled.

As he turned the corner heading north, Jack admired the large, colorful "save the date" poster in the Chamber of Commerce window. Every year the Chamber sponsored an autumn event to recognize businesses that had a positive impact on the community. A few weeks ago, the Chamber Director had notified Jack that the Chamber wished to honor and recognize the hospital this year. To that end, a committee had been formed to plan a middle school science festival to encourage young people to pursue the sciences.

"Maybe one of the middle school students will be a doctor here someday," the Director had told Jack.

"Let's hope," Jack had replied.

Still slowly pedaling, Jack grinned as he thought of the science festival planning committee meeting he had attended just last evening. Mrs. Gavery, a popular middle school science teacher, had brought three 6th grade students to present a theme idea.

The three 6th graders were dressed in full bumble bee costumes and carrying large, brightly colored plastic flowers on sticks. One student held a large sign with the lettering covered by a plastic garbage bag.

"The girls would like to share what we've been learning," Mrs. Gavery said as the eight committee members were seated in their chairs. "Go ahead, girls."

"Bees need nectar from flowers for food," the first girl began.

"Did you know that when bees land in a flower to eat, they get pollen on their bodies and that rubs off on the next flower?" the second student said. "That makes more flowers for the future."

She continued, "To survive, the bees need the flowers, and the flowers need the bees."

"Just like the hospital needs the town, and the town needs the hospital," the girls announced together.

Mrs. Gavery nodded and the girls unveiled the lettering on the sign:

Where would our community BEE without our hospital?

Committee members laughed and clapped. They had their theme. "And where would the hospital BEE without the community?" Jack said, laughing with everyone else. He was still chuckling when the three bumble bees handed him the sign and a flower so they could all pose for a photo.

"What a clever idea," he said, looking at the students. "No doubt our town works better when we stick together."

Little did Jack know that at that very moment, a piece of paper rolled out of a hospital printer that would threaten to tear the community apart.

Jack was still grinning at the memory when he parked his front tire into the hospital bike rack. He noticed the engraved plastic sign attached to the rack that said "Proudly Donated in Appreciation for the Hospital from Wally's Ski and Sports."

Yet another example of the connected bee and flower, he thought.

Jack headed into the employee door. No need to lock the bike around here.

Walking down the employee entrance hallway, Jack smiled and greeted employees by name as everyone moved swiftly to start the day. Colleagues scurried to move large carts of supplies draped in sterile plastic coverings to some destination while the housekeeping team mopped and sterilized. Surgical staff bustled through the area, concentrating on the next patient case and taking care of details along the way.

Jack wound his way to the public hallway and entered the main lobby. Most patients in the waiting area were elderly, either accompanied by an adult child or some other caregiver. Colleagues registered each patient as quickly as possible and then arranged for an escort to take that person to the correct department.

Most patients were addressed by name, yet needed to offer name and birthdate officially as part of the safety verification process.

Several pharmaceutical and medical equipment representatives already sat in lobby room chairs reviewing materials and waiting for the opportunity to meet a clinician. Most sipped morning beverages offered by the lobby coffee shop, a corner gathering spot operated by the popular and generous husband/wife couple who also owned the coffee shop downtown.

Jack stopped walking to look out the large lobby window. A semi-trailer truck housing the mobile MRI service turned onto hospital property. Because rural hospitals generally did not see enough patients to purchase multi-million dollar pieces of equipment, mobile services were the typical solution. This meant specially-outfitted semi-trailers arrived on a regular rotation year round. Mobile services were a welcome sight, because that meant more services provided locally and more revenue generated.

Unfortunately for the driver of the rig, this would not be his day. As he turned the large truck left to access the parking pad for the day, the driver turned too sharply and the trailer struck a large hospital sign. A corner of the sign broke off and the sign was bent backward at an odd angle.

The truck driver stopped immediately and climbed out of the cab, shaking his head. To add insult to injury, Jack and a number of patients were looking through the lobby window and had seen everything.

Jack was dialing his cell phone to call Rich in maintenance when he saw Rich walking quickly toward the cab. With Rich providing hand signals, the driver slowly repositioned the truck to get around the damaged sign.

Jack was pleased to let Rich deal with this relatively minor problem. The situation would require some paperwork and sign repair, but there were no injuries and no delay for scheduled patients.

Just another day, Jack thought.

Chapter Three

The $100 Rural Hospital

Jack stood in Gary's office doorway. The two men had adjacent offices in the administration hallway, so conversations were easy and free flowing. Most days involved multiple visits back and forth, which built a comfortable camaraderie between them.

Gary had been the hospital's Chief Financial Officer for over fifteen years. With a CFO career spanning twenty years across numerous facilities, Gary had wide healthcare financial experience and a long memory.

"$100?" Jack asked.

"Yes," Gary answered. "Seriously."

"That's hard to imagine. Wow," Jack said, shaking his head.

Gary had just shared an article circulating through the national healthcare headlines. Closed rural hospitals across America were being purchased by an investor group for $100 each. The total purchase price included the land, building, and all equipment and furnishings that remained in the facility.

"Have you ever seen anything like that?" Jack asked.

"Never," was Gary's one word reply.

Silent pause.

"What will investors do with an empty hospital after they buy it?" Jack asked.

"Either sell off whatever they can and keep the difference," Gary replied. "Or open some profitable service without the requirements of a hospital license, I would guess."

"Or maybe they just play landlord by fixing up the facility and leasing to someone," Gary added.

"That could be us one day," Jack said.

Gary shook his head. "We're a long way from that, Jack, so don't obsess on it," he said. "I only mentioned it because the headline had caught my attention."

Gary knew this was the sort of thing that his boss would overanalyze. Jack himself would agree. Jack had worked his adult life to control anxiety and urges to catastrophize. From a distance people saw Jack as a picture of accomplishment, calm and stability. Yet that progress was years in the making and required constant attention. Jack's first instinct was to complete everything himself and do whatever it took to please everyone. Genetic predisposition? The need to control? Difficulties coping with triggers? Some combination? Jack didn't know the exact cause. What he did know was that he worked every day to manage his own thought processes and responses to stressful situations.

Ninety seconds, he would remind himself when needed. *Pausing ninety seconds is the difference between a reaction and a reasoned response.*

"How many of these hospitals have sold for $100?" Jack asked.

"Eleven facilities in five states so far," Gary replied. "Sounds like more purchases are on the way."

"We're always on the financial edge here, Gary," Jack said. "It may be a long shot, but ending up in the $100 discount bin isn't impossible."

Gary shrugged.

"Either way, the timing of our meeting in a few minutes is a funny coincidence, yes?" Jack said.

Gary smiled. "Yep. Sometimes you can't make this stuff up."

In one hour Jack and Gary would host an informational meeting in the hospital conference room. Administrative representatives and a Chancellor from the County had asked for a meeting because they had some questions about hospital financial operations.

There were years of history between the hospital and elected county leaders. When Jack had asked about the hospital and county relationship during his Board of Trustee interview, Merrill had grinned and said, "Have you ever heard of the Hatfields and McCoys?"

Let's hope today's meeting goes better than usual, Jack thought.

Susan Larger, Phil Reckersen and Betty Langrit had poured themselves a cup of coffee from two carafes placed in the hospital community conference room when Jack and Gary entered the room. With ten minutes to go before the scheduled meeting time, Jack still apologized for being late. He would have preferred to have been there to greet the trio on arrival as a courtesy.

Susan and Phil served in elected administrative roles and Betty was an elected Chancellor. Lifelong residents of the county, each had raised their families in the area and all three spent long hours attending to county business. Susan and Phil had been re-elected once, and Betty had won re-election three times.

"Thanks for coming, folks," Jack began after everyone had been seated around a long rectangular conference table. "Betty, when you called, you mentioned some questions about hospital finances."

"Thanks for meeting with us, Jack and Gary," Betty said. "I'll get right to the point. We're hearing that the hospital has taken out a large loan and we think that action should have come before the County Chancellors before being approved. If it happened, it probably wasn't legal."

What the hell? Jack thought.

Susan added, "We know the hospital has lots of financial challenges, so we also think you should be getting permission from the county before any equipment purchases or signing any contractual commitments."

Susan, Phil and Betty looked at Jack, waiting for an answer.

Ninety seconds, Jack said to himself. *Ninety seconds.*

Jack cleared his throat. He wished he would have invited Merrill. It would have been appropriate for the hospital Board Chair to be part of this conversation.

"Where are these questions coming from?" Jack asked. "I'm sure no one here needs a reminder that the hospital is a separate entity and already has a publicly-elected Board of Trustees."

Phil nodded. "That may be, but I'm sure you've noticed that we have a small group of people who attend every County Chancellor meeting and question everything we do."

Phil continued, "When I say everything, I mean *everything*. Even the number of miles between two towns if one of us requests mileage reimbursement. That alone could be a 10-minute argument in some meetings."

Susan said, "Really this request is to help you. If you bring your topics to the Chancellor meetings for approval, we'll know what's going on and have better answers."

"Look, there's so much wrong here I hardly know where to start," Jack said. "First, the hospital hasn't taken out any large new loans. And besides, even if it did, the hospital Board of Trustees has clear authority to do that. And don't forget the Board follows open meetings laws to the letter, so every action is available to the community. So let's stop this 'it isn't legal' crap right now because that's ridiculous."

Gary gave Jack a look that said *tone it down.*

"The sad part is that this county does not provide a penny of on-going tax support to the hospital. Unlike almost every other county in the state," Jack added.

"That's a whole different issue," Susan said sharply.

"Is it?" Jack shot back. "You said our topic is about hospital financial performance and let me tell you, other hospitals have a huge advantage because they get hundreds of thousands, if not millions, of dollars per year to fund hospital operations."

"Well, that's not going to happen in this county," said Susan. "You know as well as I do that there is a long history around here, and the southern half of the county will not support money going to the northern half. So please drop it."

Jack continued, "As far as the idea that every piece of equipment or contract needs review by the county, drop that. This facility is not owned by the county. Plain and simple," he said. "What are you thinking we would do? Have a hospital Board meeting, get approval, and then schedule a County Chancellor meeting to get approval for the same thing? Would we need approval to buy staples? How about paper clips?"

"Let's refill our coffee cups, everyone," Gary said as he rose from his seat to find a coffee carafe. He shot a look at Jack that said *knock it off.*

Betty said, "No thank you, Gary." She looked at Jack. "So you don't like our requests, Jack. Then how do you suggest we answer the naysayers at every meeting?"

"That's exactly my point," Jack said. "Why are you worrying about placating the naysayers, the people you will *never* please, instead of finding ways to support the hospital that is the healthcare and economic engine of the county?"

No answer. An awkward, silent pause.

"Obviously we see all of this differently," Betty said.

"No doubt," Jack replied. "But since you took the time to visit, at least let me share four important numbers about the hospital: One thousand. Two hundred fifty. $15 million and $46 million."

Susan, Phil and Betty were intrigued and listening.

Jack continued, "First, one thousand. Together the hospital, clinics and all departments have over one thousand patient interactions *per week*. That's a good chunk of the entire county population receiving care from the organization every seven days."

"Next, two hundred fifty. There are two hundred fifty full-time employees. That's around seven hundred family members who depend on the hospital for employment. And those employees live in every town and township across the entire county."

Jack left no room for interruptions. "Now $15 million. That's the payroll per year, far beyond any other employer in the county," he said. "Consider $15 million paid to hospital employees, then those employees spend those dollars at local stores, hair salons, restaurants, daycare - you name it."

Jack paused to take a quick sip of coffee. "Last is $46 million. The hospital pays retail sales taxes, attracts other tax paying entities and circulates its own dollars through the county. Studies suggest this hospital adds $46 million of positive economic activity to the county economy *every year*."

"Those are certainly interesting numbers, Jack," Betty said. "We appreciate you sharing that information."

"I just don't get it," Jack continued. "Every county in America, including this one, is working to recruit new businesses," he said. "How would this county ever recruit a new business to replace the positive impact the hospital has *right now*?"

Susan and Phil began to gather papers they had set on the table. Betty thought before replying.

"Jack, please know we are just asking questions and trying to do the best for our constituents," Betty said. "So don't take it personally."

Too late, Jack thought.

"Having said that, I know I really appreciated learning those facts and figures about the hospital, so thank you," Betty added. Susan and Phil said nothing.

By now everyone was standing and Phil stood with his hand on the door handle.

Deep down, Jack appreciated all three of the county public servants. He fully recognized they each had a difficult job trying to keep everyone happy. Jack understood that feeling. And he knew that in the end, every person in that room was simply trying to do the best they could for the community.

"I have one more number for you to remember today," Jack said. "$100. Because apparently closed rural hospitals in America are selling for $100 these days."

Raised eyebrows and surprise. Without another word, Phil opened the door and the three visitors left the room.

Jack and Gary let the trio show themselves to the hospital front door.

Chapter 4

Just a Regular Day

8:17 am that Friday. Jack finished listening to a brief morning state hospital association advocacy conference call. Over the next few months the association would be advocating for more rural facility funding, a constant priority to meet chronic financial pressures.

Normally Jack tried to keep his schedule light on Fridays. Any given week, the days were filled with back-to-back meetings with employees, medical staff, community members, peer organizations or telephone calls. Most weeks there would be a meeting at least two evenings per week.

Fridays were good days to catch up with paperwork and spend more time visiting with employees. Mondays would return to the normal series of back-to-back meetings, anyway.

Jack's calendar had only three commitments that day, two in the morning and one over lunch. The first was a routine morning meeting with a hospital department head and the second was a brief presentation as guest speaker to the local women's quilters guild. That meeting would be convenient because the group met in the hospital community conference room. The third meeting would be a lunchtime presentation downtown to a joint meeting of the local Rotary Club and Jaycees Club.

Because Gary was out of the office, the administrative team for the day were Jack and Connie Kemper, an extremely capable administrative office professional.

She stepped into Jack's doorway holding a box of staples. "Good morning," she said as she leaned forward and placed the box into his desk tray. "Any big plans for the weekend?"

"Just a couple things," Jack replied. "The Walk the Talk fundraiser event in the morning, and then we work the concession stand at the afternoon volleyball game."

Visibility at local events is a key part of any rural hospital CEO life and Jack and Amy enjoyed the chance to attend, especially since Charlie was getting old enough to participate.

"How about you? How is your mom doing?" Jack asked. Connie's elderly mother had recently moved in with her.

"Well, we're doing the best we can," she said. Connie was pulled in many directions caring for her mother, assisting her adult children, and helping now and then with her grandchildren.

"Let us know how we can help," Jack said.

"Will do. Thank you. And remember, it's just the two of us here today to cover telephones," Connie reminded Jack.

"Sounds good," Jack replied as he ventured down the hallway headed for the meeting with the department head. It started in 90 seconds.

In a small rural hospital, Jack had plenty of time to get there.

Later that morning Jack was speaking before eighteen quilters guild members in the community conference room.

He shared several patient care stories and was wrapping up with a brief financial update, "...we are working hard to improve the financial condition of the hospital. While we lost money last month and last fiscal year, we have a number of positive developments underway that should make a difference."

Jack ended with a request for their help.

"We need a favor," he asked. "When you need care for yourself or a family member, please remember we have an outstanding clinic with family medicine physicians and other providers. We have an inpatient unit, a 24-hour emergency department and a general surgery department," Jack continued. "We also replace hips and knees and our local clinic has outstanding family medicine physicians. And of course we deliver babies here, too."

The ladies smiled and nodded at that thought. "We love making quilts for the little ones," the guild president said proudly. "And the baby section in the hospital Gift Shop is darling."

"Thank you. I will pass that along," Jack answered. "And please know that everyone at the hospital really appreciates everything your group does for us."

His time on their schedule was complete and he did not want to overstay his welcome. With a wave and thumbs up, Jack made his way to the door. Time to head to the parking lot for the two minute drive downtown for the lunchtime service club presentation.

Chapter 5

The Letter

3:13 pm. Jack was back in his office getting ready to finish the day. Lightly skimming various emails while softly streaming music on his phone, he did easy tasks to finish the week.

The main administration door latch clicked and a familiar local physician entered the office hallway. Dr. Smith was a 40-something physician who personally delivered 98% of all babies born at the facility. Basically the entire obstetrics service and all related services and staff surrounding the program depended on him.

Jack came from behind his desk with a hearty greeting. "Hello, Dr. Smith!"

Dr. Smith gave a feeble smile but did not make eye contact and seemed uncharacteristically nervous.

"I need to give you this. Nothing personal, but it's time," he said as he handed Jack a white envelope. "And don't try to talk me out of it, because you can't."

Without another word, Dr. Smith turned around swiftly and headed for the door. "We'll talk soon," Jack said with fake cheeriness as the door slowly swung closed.

Connie had seen Dr. Smith come and go quickly so she left her office and stepped into the hallway.

"What was that all about?" she asked.

Jack tore open the envelope and skimmed the letter:

...please accept my resignation from the facility effective 90 days from the date of this letter...

Without Dr. Smith, in 90 days the facility had no obstetrics service and no local physician to deliver babies.

Jack handed the letter to Connie.

"Don't say anything to anyone about this yet," he said.

Connie read the letter with a solemn look on her face.

"Oh my," she said. "This is going to be a big deal."

After sitting quietly in his office lost in thought for a while, Jack packed his work bag, preparing to leave for the weekend. He had folded the letter and put it in the back of his top desk drawer.

His mind raced. *People will think this is my fault. What will this mean for my career? Why didn't Dr. Smith say something earlier? I let everybody down. What about employees? People are going to lose their jobs. I don't want to tell anyone the bad news. No one else has to deal with these tough issues - other hospital CEOs have it easy. What happens to expecting mothers? This will make the newspaper for sure. These days, it will probably be national news. We'll never find another doctor to do deliveries in our small town. People have no idea how hard and expensive it is to run that service. What will it take to get Dr. Smith to rescind his resignation? Will someone ask for my resignation? What will my Board Chair think?*

One final irony dawned on Jack. *Wow, the quilters guild just told me how much they loved having babies delivered here.*

Jack continued the negative self-talk walking to the parking lot. His thoughts shifted to the Board Chair and Chief of the Medical Staff.

I'll wait to call Merrill. He's the Board Chair and he hired me to solve problems, not dump problems on him on Friday afternoon, Jack thought. *Dr. Molson is probably busy seeing patients, so I'll wait to call him.*

When Jack pulled into his garage, he could hear Charlie pitching a fit as Amy tried to console him. At least that was a distraction for a while. The evening passed into the next day as the family went to the fundraiser and volleyball event.

Jack didn't mention the letter to Amy the entire weekend. He didn't want to talk about it.

Chapter 6

Roadblocks and Dead Ends

Monday morning, Jack sat at his desk holding his telephone. He had called the larger health system affiliated with his critical access hospital. Over the weekend, Jack had convinced himself that the system affiliate partner would have capacity to place an obstetrics provider locally in the community.

"Jack, you know we've supported the community for years, if not decades," the physician leader of the obstetrics group said. "But this is crisis time for obstetrics across the United States, and we're no different. We simply do not have any physicians who can cover your community 24/7/365."

Jack drew a deep breath and let it go slowly.

The physician continued, "I hate to tell you, but we are simply not an option and we won't be an option for the foreseeable future," he said. "Sorry about that."

The voice on the other end of the telephone sounded tired. Jack completely understood. Obstetrics volumes were increasing in urban areas and the physician had probably been up all night delivering babies.

"I understand, Doctor," Jack said. "Thank you for your time and candor."

They both hung up.

Jack knew of another OB/GYN physician group located about 60 miles away. He had the telephone number, so he placed the next call immediately.

Jack told the receptionist that he would wait as long as necessary for Dr. Melee, the lead physician, to answer his page. Dr. Melee was an experienced OB/GYN physician and his practice drew patients from a wide geographic area. With eight OB/GYN providers, Jack was hopeful the group somehow had time and desire to cover his hospital.

"This Dr. Melee," said the voice on the line.

"Dr. Melee, this is Jack McGee. I am the administrator…" Jack began.

"I remember you. How can I help?" Dr. Melee was in a hurry.

"I received a resignation from the local physician who does the majority of obstetrics deliveries in our community and wondered if your group would consider expanding services to provide coverage here."

Dr. Melee didn't hesitate. "I appreciate the call, but that will not be possible. Our patient volumes are bursting at the seams right now and we just lost a candidate we thought would sign to join us. Another partner is trying to phase into retirement, so as much as I hate to say it, we can't help."

His tone made it clear, so Jack didn't object, "I understand, Dr. Melee." Jack answered. "Thank you for your time on a busy Monday morning. "Jack put the telephone on his desk.

He sat there staring vacantly, shoulders slumped.

Connie poked her head in Jack's office. "I'll bet it was a long weekend for you," she said. "What did Dr. Molson and Merrill say?"

Jack hadn't contacted either one of them yet.

Connie raised her eyebrows. She simply turned and disappeared from his office doorway.

Jack shrugged and headed down the hallway toward the routine Monday morning staff huddle.

When Jack returned to his office, Connie was waiting for him. "I hate to overstep my bounds," she started.

Jack looked at her.

"Shouldn't you call Dr. Molson and Merrill so they aren't caught off guard?" she asked.

"Not until I get some more information," Jack said.

Connie slowly shook her head and returned to her office.

Jack dialed a telephone number and waited.

"Jack, great to hear from you. How have you been?" said a female voice with a deep Southern accent. Mary Jess owned a physician recruiting firm in New Orleans. Jack had met Mary about five years ago and she always managed to solve his physician recruiting challenges.

"Not so well, Mary," Jack said. "The physician who delivered 98% of the babies here has resigned with 90 days notice, so we need coverage ASAP. Given the tight timing, I assume we'll need temporary coverage on day ninety-one until a permanent replacement can be found."

Mary whistled. "That's going to be a tall order, Jack," she said. "Obstetrics physicians are hard to place in rural communities, and it gets tougher every day."

"Just to get a ballpark cost idea," Jack asked. "If we signed for a temporary physician on day ninety one, what would that cost?"

"We just did an obstetrics fill-in at a western critical access hospital, so let me take a look to confirm my memory," Jack heard clicking sounds as Mary searched her computer database.

"Ouch. Twenty-six hundred dollars per day, plus travel, food, and lodging," Mary said. "So of course the financial result depends on how many babies your hospital will deliver."

"Our patient volumes won't be nearly enough to cover that," Jack said. "How long would it take to recruit and place a permanent obstetrics physician to our community?"

Mary whistled again. "Wow, that's hard to say, Jack. I saw an article recently that said some rural communities are becoming obstetrics 'deserts' because the resources are drying up. IF we could find a physician, and that is a big IF, it could take a year or more. But even then, I can't say for sure. In my twenty-two years recruiting physicians, bringing obstetric physicians to rural areas is about as difficult as I have seen."

Jack was quiet. What he had heard made him nervous.

"Should I start looking for a physician for you?" she asked.

"Not yet," Jack replied. "I don't know what we're going to do just yet. Give me a little time."

As Jack hung up his telephone, there was a knock on his office door.

"Got a minute?" Dr. John Molson, the Chief of the Medical Staff, let himself in.

"Dr. Smith just told me that he has resigned effective in 90 days," Dr. Molson said, pacing in front of Jack's desk.

"Yes," Jack said.

"Don't you think you could have said something to me?" Dr. Molson said. "You had all weekend to call or text me with a heads up. Nothing from you."

Dr. Molson continued, "So this morning I was completely shell-shocked. Just think what this means for patients. For the community. We need an emergency meeting of the Medical Staff today to start talking about this."

"Not to mention the staff. They are down there right now buzzing, and you haven't said one word," Dr. Molson added.

"Well, this morning I called a large obstetrics group and a physician recruiter to get started," Jack's answer sounded weak, and he knew it.

Disgusted, Dr. Molson shook his head and paced right out Jack's door.

"We need to get on this now!" he said as he left the area.

Jack's phone buzzed with a text. "Call me." It was from Merrill Stricker, the Board Chair.

"What's going on over there?" Merrill demanded. Jack had never heard Merrill's voice like this. Angry and disappointed at the same time.

"I've already taken three calls this morning. One from Dr. Molson and two from nurses in the obstetrics unit. They told me Dr. Smith is leaving and you haven't said anything."

"Dr. Smith resigned with 90 days notice on Friday afternoon," Jack said.

"Why didn't you call me to let me know?" Merrill asked. "I would have appreciated the heads up."

Jack's stomach fell.

"I was trying to figure out alternatives before saying anything. I thought I could get some answers before reaching out," Jack said.

"Pretty naive, Jack," Merrill asked. "You know how small this world is. Did you expect Dr. Smith to stay silent?"

That would have been nice, Jack thought.

"Not really," was all Jack could say.

A pause on the other end of the line.

"So what's your plan now?" Merrill asked.

"I'll call the other Board members right now to give them a heads up," Jack said. "Then I'll walk through the obstetrics unit to speak with the staff."

"You'd better plan on a call from the newspaper," Merrill said. "Those nurses are mad and told me the hospital isn't doing anything to keep obstetrics services."

"That's not true," Jack said. "I'm already on it."

"Do they know that?" Merrill asked.

"No, I guess not," Jack replied.

"Keep me posted on all of this," Merrill said.

"I wi–" Jack started to respond. Merrill had hung up.

Jack walked to the cafeteria to fill his cup of coffee before calling the other Board members. Rather than the usual upbeat "hello!" or "good morning!" in the hallways, employees avoided eye contact with him or curtly said hello.

Doesn't take long for word to spread, Jack thought to himself.

"Thanks for your time. I agree, it's not good. More to come. Bye," Jack hung up the phone and finished his last Board member telephone call. At least now the Board members knew the problem. One other Board member had already heard the news and let Jack know loudly and clearly that he was upset by the "ambush," as he had called it.

I probably won't even get a decent job recommendation now, Jack thought to himself.

Telephone messages had been accumulating on the magnet outside his office door, his voice mail light was blinking, and he had received nearly thirty emails. He had around fifteen new texts on his cell phone.

Jack had responded to nothing. He had made Board member calls. And spent time looking out his window.

Jack's phone buzzed again. Gary was texting from his office next door.

Read the online media story as soon as you can.

Jack opened his web browser and went to the local media website. A large Breaking News banner scrolled across the top of the webpage. *Obstetrics Physician to Leave Community* ran the headline. *Future of obstetrics deliveries in doubt* was the sub-headline.

Jack read the story. Written entirely from the view of Dr. Smith and several unnamed obstetrics nurses, the story was factual and had no inaccuracies.

The hospital had no comment, the story read.

Jack checked his email. An urgent email request for comment from the local editor. He checked his text: an urgent text from over an hour ago from the editor requesting comment. He poked his head out the door and pulled the stack of pink slips with telephone messages: a telephone message from the editor.

He has tried to reach me, Jack thought. *The "no comment" looks like I am trying to hide something.*

Jack glanced at his computer monitor again. Three emails from medical staff members asking what was going on with obstetrics and Dr. Smith. Dr. Molson had texted twice asking Jack to call, but Jack continued to ignore the messages.

His door had been closed for nearly two hours. Finally Jack chose to dial the obstetrics department at the state University. An alumni of the University, located some seventy miles away, Jack knew there were dozens of obstetrics physicians practicing in the University system and hoped somehow he could arrange coverage.

The receptionist on the line was accommodating. She promised to hand-deliver Jack's phone message to the department chair. Just a short while later, Jack's cell phone rang.

"This is Jack McGee," he answered.

"Hello, Mr. McGee. This is Dr. Joshi, Chair of the obstetrics unit. I have a message to call you because you're looking for coverage at a critical access hospital."

"Yes, sir," Jack replied. "Our top delivering physician has resigned with 90 days notice, so we are looking for both temporary or long-term coverage. Any way we could meet to discuss any possibilities?"

"Thank you kindly for thinking of our department, Mr. McGee. But I am afraid that will be quite impossible. Patient demands here go beyond our physician capacity, so we cannot accommodate any outside requests," Dr. Joshi explained.

"Do you see the possibilities changing in the near future?" Jack asked.

"Candidly, no, I regret to say that it will be even more difficult to accommodate a request like this in the future," Dr. Joshi replied.

"Thank you very much for your time, Sir," Jack said as he hung up.

He shook his head. Dead end after dead end.

How is this going to look to everyone? went the self-talk as Jack blinked back tears.

Connie met Jack in the hallway as he left his office. "Jack, there are lots of rumors floating around and people are getting anxious wondering what will happen now that Dr. Smith has resigned," she said. "Have you considered calling a manager meeting to let department heads know what's going on?"

Jack shook his head. "I'm going to leave the building for a while, Connie. So no, I don't plan to call a manager meeting today."

Jack headed for the door.

Amy knew something had happened because Jack was home unexpectedly in the middle of the afternoon, but the only answer she could get was "I don't want to talk about it." Charlie was napping so Jack went downstairs and turned on the television.

Jack resurfaced for dinner, made small talk with Amy and then offered to clean up the dishes. Amy played with Charlie while Jack filled the dishwasher.

"Should we go for a walk with Charlie when you finish?" Amy asked. "Fresh air might do you some good."

"No thanks," Jack answered. "I want to call Jim Ware. I'm hoping he can arrange for some of his obstetrics physicians to provide coverage here."

Amy nodded and put Charlie in the stroller.

"We'll be back later," she said. "Hang in there, honey. We love you."

Jack smiled as he dialed Jim's number.

Jim Ware was Jack's best friend from graduate school. Jim was the CEO of a large multi-specialty physician group in a large, affluent growing urban community about eighty-one miles from Jack's community.

"Our OBs are pretty busy as it is," Jim said after Jack had explained the dilemma. "In fact, we just signed four more docs to join the group later this year with two more committed next year after their residency. That's how fast we're growing."

"Sounds like you are in a great situation, Jim." Jack said, trying to sound cheerful.

"Hmmm," Jim said. For a moment, Jack's hopes rose.

"I'm just wondering. How does the obstetrics call schedule work there with so few physicians?" Jim asked. "Are the OBs on call about every other day?"

"Yes," Jack answered. "Sometimes seven days a week."

"Wow," Jim exclaimed. "Our group is so large OB physicians take call just one time per month."

Brief pause in the conversation.

"Sorry I can't help you, man," Jim said.

"I understand, of course," Jack said. "Just thought I would ask."

"Good luck, buddy," Jim said. "Hey, sometime the two of us need to get away to the new condo my wife and I just bought in Colorado. It's right at the base of the mountain and the ski slope leads right to the hot tub on our back deck. You'll love it."

I'm sure I will, Jack thought to himself.

It was 7:00 am and Jack was waiting in the hallway outside Dr. Mia Soderland's office.

Awake half the previous night, his feeling of desperation was growing as the options to replace Dr. Smith were evaporating one by one. He didn't want to be there this morning, but owed it to the patients to ask.

Dr. Soderland was a family medicine physician who saw patients two days per week in her office and still delivered babies locally for select patients.

Last year Dr. Soderland had delivered five babies at the local hospital. She took no call coverage for other physicians and attended medical staff meetings only to meet the required minimum for membership. Even though she practiced in the community, she admitted no patients to the hospital and referred patients for ancillary services very rarely, even if patients specifically requested otherwise.

Five months ago during an unrelated obstetrics conversation at the hospital Medical Staff meeting, Dr. Soderland had let it be known that she did not want to grow the obstetrics portion of her practice.

"I will do no additional deliveries, do I make myself clear?" she had said.

"Very clear," Dr. Molson, the Medical Staff Chair had answered.

That particular morning Dr. Soderland saw Jack when she turned into the hallway to get to her office. Jack smiled and said "good morning." No answer.

She stepped past Jack and pressed the four-digit code to unlock her office door. Placing her bag on her desk, she said as she turned around, "So you finally ran Dr. Smith off."

The usual, Jack thought.

"Dr. Soderland, the hospital obviously needs obstetrics physician coverage to continue the service," Jack began, speaking deliberately and choosing his words carefully. "Since you already deliver a few babies a year, would you be interested in picking up additional obstetrics coverage, even in the interim, to keep the service going while we look for alternatives?"

"Absolutely not," she said. "And I assume the hospital will make arrangements so that I can continue to deliver the same number of babies I usually do."

"Well, that's up in the air right now," Jack began. "We're loo- -"

"All I get from the hospital are demands and more demands," she said, shaking her head. "Anything else? Because I'm busy."

Her biting tone and obvious dismissal stung Jack. *Why do I let her get to me like that*? he asked himself as he walked down the hallway, a lump in his throat.

It turns out, this wasn't the worst part of Jack's day.

Chapter 7

The Nighttime Nadir

9:19 pm that same evening. Pitch dark outside. No moon. No stars. A cloudy, windy, dreary day had deteriorated to an evening of loud wind gusts splattering rain against Jack's office window. It was cold outside with temperatures around 38 degrees and destined to sink throughout the night.

Jack's day had started at 7 am. Fourteen hours later he had yet to leave the facility. Over the past few weeks, every single option to replace Dr. Smith had failed. Even if there were providers, there was not enough money. And even if there was enough money, there were not enough providers.

This evening Jack was in his office alone, and he *felt* alone.

Not only alone, but Jack felt *responsible.*

Negative self-talk, not helpful yet never far away, played like a constant stream in his mind: *This is my fault. Why can't I find an obstetric doctor to fill the schedule? Should I resign? Will I get fired? There are easier ways to make a living. Failure.*

Disheartened and staring at the landline telephone on his desk, Jack was shaking his head and said out loud: "$3,000 per day."

Out loud again, with sarcasm he said, "Gee, that's only $21,000 per week. No problem."

He had just hung up the telephone after a scheduled call with yet another overpromising physician recruiter claiming he was ready to commit a contract and recruit quality obstetrics physicians.

For a mere $3,000 fee per day, plus travel, food, and lodging.

Earlier that day Jack had reviewed preliminary hospital financial results for the previous month. Not good. Another operating loss added to the operating loss the previous month, added to the operating loss the previous month, added to the operating loss the month before that.

Those financial reports were painful because the consequences were so real. And the negative numbers were getting bigger and bigger every month.

The same vintage battery-powered pocket calculator had lived on Jack's work desk every location and stage of his career. He had kept that thing for years and it showed.

Jack multiplied the daily fee times 365 days.

"For a rotating circuit of different obstetrics physicians every week to air-drop into the community to be available to deliver babies," he said to his empty office. "Just what we want for our patients."

Why stop now? Time to jot numbers onto a piece of scratch paper to estimate the total yearly costs to deliver babies at the facility. Nothing specific, just a guesstimate.

Jack started a list: a fill-in obstetrics physician at $3,000 per day; at least that much for a surgeon contract for c-section back-up; a family medicine physician; staff members; equipment; supplies and everything else it takes for a service to deliver babies at a facility.

Jack pressed so hard making the list that he broke the pencil lead, twice.

Consider the average number of babies born per year at the facility, and presto! The result is a million dollar loss per year for the service. Even with an increased number of deliveries, which was not guaranteed, the losses were staggering.

Tonight all options seemed to be drying up. Along with Jack's hope.

Ironically, earlier that evening the recruitment representative had ended their conversation saying they were pleased to offer a "solution" to the situation.

Solution, my ass, Jack thought. *Not even close.*

He just stared at his calculator.

Three hard knocks on the administration door.

At this hour? Who could that be? Jack asked himself. Any employee would have a badge to swipe for entry and no visitor should have access to the lobby after 9:00 pm.

The administration office suite door was solid wood with no windows and locked automatically at 6:00 pm every evening.

Jack couldn't see the visitor, but without a thought he pressed the button and the automatic hydraulic hinge slowly opened.

"Are you the boss here?" a well-dressed woman around thirty years of age with striking brown eyes and wire-rimmed glasses asked Jack somberly.

She was wet from being outside in the rainstorm, yet made no effort to dry herself or adjust her hair. Jack did not recognize her and wondered how she had accessed this area of the building. Jack assumed she was a family member of an inpatient and wanted directions to find her way out of the building.

"I guess that's me," Jack replied. "How may I help?"

She drew a large breath and said, "I just had to come here. I came into town to walk through the obstetrics unit again. And talk to you."

You had to come here tonight? How did you know I would be here? Jack thought to himself.

He motioned for her to step forward into the empty main hospital lobby area and pointed toward two chairs. "Shall we sit down?" Jack asked.

Jack and the woman sat with one empty chair between them.

She looked directly at Jack. "I've been reading and hearing from friends that you're trying to close the obstetrics unit and stop deliveries here," she began.

Jack's shoulders fell.

See? People think it's your fault, said his inner voice.

Jack shook his head. "We're working day and night to find an obstetrics physician to fill the schedule."

"My daughter was delivered here a little over three years ago," she continued. "Dr. Smith and the nurses were fantastic."

"It's nice to hear you had a good experience, but…" Jack was not sure where she was going with all this.

Her tone hardened. "I'm pregnant, and I'm going to do everything I can to stop you because I want to deliver my baby here like I did before."

"This isn't about 'stopping me'," Jack made air quotes with both hands. "In fact I'm still here tonight trying to recruit a doctor."

"If you close the unit, won't you even feel bad about the mothers who can't travel for their appointments?" she interrupted.

Tears welled up in Jack's eyes. "Of course," he answered. "More than you can imagine. That's why we're trying to…"

Another interruption: "What about the jobs you're going to cut?" she said. "Think of the nurses and their families."

Every time she said "you," Jack felt defensive. And hurt.

Why would this woman come to the hospital this late in the evening during a storm? How did she get in? How did she know I was in my office? Jack was befuddled.

Before Jack could respond to her question, across the large lobby he could see one of the inpatient nurses aides walking toward them.

Jack recognized Sheila Frank. She was a strong presence on the floor, voicing her opinion and often stopping Jack with several questions each morning during his administrative walk-abouts.

Jack was glad to see Sheila because it might interrupt the odd exchange underway with this stranger.

Nodding and smiling toward Sheila as she approached, Jack assumed Sheila would walk over to address the visitor or join the conversation somehow. Instead, Sheila paused about five feet away and put her hands on her hips, not saying a word.

Then it dawned on him: she was there to listen to the conversation.

Now with an audience of one, the visitor did not wait for Jack to respond and continued, "Mark my words: even if you cut the service, babies will be born in this facility. You just won't be ready for them. Your emergency room had better get ready."

No pause. She's on a roll.

"Is it all about the money?" she continued. "Why does everything need to be about money?"

Jack simply looked at her.

"What's next? Do you plan to close the whole hospital?" she asked. "We never know because everything is always secret and behind closed doors around here."

"Absolutely false," Jack heard himself say. "I don't know where you heard that, but that's 100% false."

She leaned forward in her chair. "We've started an online petition demanding the obstetrics unit stay open and we already have 260 signatures," she said. "Our goal is 1,000 signatures and then we'll present the petition to the Board."

Jack stood up.

"Ok, ma'am," Jack announced. "I didn't even get your name. I'm Jack McGee, but I assume you know that. I don't know how you got in here, but I've certainly heard enough for tonight."

"My name is Heather Wyler," she said.

"Are you from here in town?" Jack asked.

"I live south of town," Heather replied.

Nurses aide Sheila was still listening. Jack motioned with his hand back and forth between the two women.

"I get it. You two know each other," Jack said. "The show's over, Sheila. Please get back to caring for your patients on the floor." Sheila nodded without a word and walked back toward the inpatient wing.

"And Heather, I'm going to walk you to the front door," Jack said matter-of-factly.

Jack hoped she wouldn't refuse to leave because there was no security guard in the small hospital. His only choice would have been to call the police.

"Fine," she answered as she stood up.

Jack and Healther walked silently side-by-side to the front entrance. Sleet slid down the window and wind gusts burst against the glass every now and then.

Jack keyed the code to open a side door and motioned for Heather to leave.

She stepped through the doorway and into the stormy black night. Jack locked the door behind her and debated whether he should walk her to her car.

He chose to walk back toward his office, figuring Heather's friends in the building would watch out for her.

Jack was back in his office, now nearly 10 pm.

No one knows the facts. People are conspiring against me. I can't believe one of our own nurses aides would do that.

Jack tried to turn his mind off while he shut down his office computer. There sat his trusty thin calculator with the large negative number in parenthesis still illuminated.

Jack grabbed the calculator and slammed it against his desk three times in quick succession. The crunch of breaking plastic sounded foreign in his office as plastic pieces flew across the room to the floor. Three smashes, now three pieces of calculator. Just one small fragment was still in his hand. Jack tossed it in the garbage can.

Another first. Jack had never done something like that at work or home before. Ever.

Jack snatched his rain jacket from the hook behind his office door and slammed the door shut behind him.

His shoulders were hunched and he hardly noticed the blowing sleet and moonless night walking to his car. He got behind the wheel and just sat in the driver's seat, rain pounding the windows and roof. He dialed his cell phone.

"Hey buddy, what's up?" Jack's lifelong friend answered the call. Friends since teenage years, both enjoyed the relationship as that friend you could call day or night.

Jack held his phone, unable to speak.

"Are you there?" came the gentle prompt.

Long pause.

Suddenly, it all poured out.

"Sorry to call you this late. So, so sorry.

"The situation here is totally out of control. The doctor that delivers babies has resigned, and I have pursued every option to replace him.

"Everything I tried has failed.

"Everyone here is unhappy and upset.

"No matter where I go in town, someone mentions this topic.

"I feel like they're blaming me like everything was fine until I showed up.

"This problem is like a huge brick I have to drag around every moment on top of the usual hassles.

"Then I put on a happy face at home so things seem normal at work, like it's not a big deal because I don't want this to affect Amy and Charlie.

"It's a problem that can't be solved the way I'm doing it.

Tears ran down Jack's face.

"With problems from all directions, right now I just run from one thing to the next.

"Then tonight one of the staff members made arrangements for some woman named Heather to come and bang on my office door and make a bunch of crazy accusations.

"I feel betrayed. Why would an employee do that? And why would this Heather feel compelled to do that?

"It feels like everything is falling apart and getting worse every day."

"I'm so sorry, buddy," came the reply.

"And now it's after 10 pm at night and I'm sitting in my damn car in a damn parking lot during a damn sleet storm in the damn pitch black trying to get my act together before I go home." Jack couldn't stop the tears.

Patient listening on the other end of the phone.

Finally Jack took a big breath and let it out slowly.

"I don't think I'm cut out for this job," Jack said. "Besides, the hospital would probably be better off having someone else lead the facility through this mess."

Chapter 8

Jack's Dad

Two weeks later. A cool and cloudy late Autumn morning. Snow will not be far away.

Jack, Amy and Charlie arrived for breakfast at the condo where Jack's Mom and Dad lived. It had been a while since they had visited due to Jack's hectic schedule. After the first round of coffee, Amy and Jack's Mom had decided to take Charlie to the library children's reading hour. This left time for another coffee and conversation between Jack and his Dad. At 66 years old, his Dad managed various health ailments yet retained his optimism and down-to-earth practicality.

After plenty of chitchat, finally, the question.

"How is work going?" Jack's Dad asked.

Pause. No answer.

"Well, that says something," his Dad said. "I know things have been hard on you lately. Your mother has noticed, too. She says your personality is changing."

Gee, that makes me feel good, Jack thought.

His Dad looked at him. "Jack, I want to ask you a question, and you need to tell me the truth."

"OK," Jack replied.

"Why did you come here today?" he asked.

"Just to see how things are going for you and Mom," Jack said. "Besides, it had been a while since you've both seen Charlie."

His Dad raised an eyebrow and looked at Jack.

At first Jack was silent. Then Jack said it out loud to his Dad.

"Because I am thinking of resigning and wondered what you thought about that."

"If that's what you really want, then I'm happy for you," he said. "But you have never been a quitter so it surprises me that you're considering that."

Tears welled up in Jack's eyes. "Everything was going along fairly well," Jack said. "And then a good situation went bad. Really bad."

"What's so bad?" his Dad asked.

"It feels like I messed it all up. I took this job and right after that the key obstetrics doctor resigned. And now everyone in town is unhappy because we can't find a way to replace that doctor to keep delivering babies the way the town always did before," Jack said.

They both sat quietly for a while.

"You've been in stressful situations before," his Dad said. "What's different here?"

"I have worked 24/7 to solve the problem and come up short with every idea," Jack said. "Everywhere I turn, I hit a brick wall."

His Dad gave Jack a familiar look that Jack had seen many times before.

"It doesn't do any good to dance around it," his Dad said. "Tell me the truth."

Jack choked up and it was hard to speak.

"I wanted to solve the problem and find a way to replace that doctor," Jack said. "Because I'm supposed to have the answers. That's why they pay me. People look to me to know what to do."

Jack went on, "I wanted to show the Board and Medical Staff and Senior Team and employees that I could take care of this."

"But with this problem, no matter how hard I try, I can't find the answer," he said.

"Keep going," his Dad prodded.

Jack drew a breath.

"I'm afraid," he finally said.

"Afraid of what?" his Dad asked.

"Failing. What others will say. The bad headlines. My career. Looking like a loser. What everyone in the family will think. What happens to the expecting mothers. Everything," Jack answered.

His Dad nodded and took a sip from his coffee mug. "I hear lots of 'I' and 'me' when you talk," he said. "*I* want the answer. *I* wanted to solve the problem. What will people think of *me*. That sort of thing."

He wasn't wrong. Jack just shrugged.

His Dad continued. "It sounds to me like you're trying to get, when instead you should be trying to give," he said.

"I don't follow," Jack said.

"You're trying to get credit by being a miracle worker when you should give up control and invite other people to help."

Jack was listening.

His Dad went on. "You've always been in it for the right reasons and you work well with others. Sure, you face a tough problem. But tough problems are when you need to see the bigger picture. Every small town has seen its share of troubles over the decades. Remember that rural folks are creative and resilient. It's just who we are," he said with a slight smile.

"But you'll never get anywhere trying to be the one who solves everything, because then you forget who you really are."

His Dad paused.

"For what it's worth, Jack, I think you're perfectly suited to lead that hospital and the town. But you need to remember who you are, and you need to help them remember who they are and what that hospital stands for."

"Right now you're operating out of fear and focusing on budgets and schedules, right?"

Jack nodded.

"That's not you, and deep down you know it."

Jack nodded again.

"Then be who you are: Teach. Listen. Show people the path. Then let go and trust the people and the process," his Dad said.

"That's the best anyone can do, pal. And we'll all love you either way."

For the first time in weeks, Jack felt his body relax.

He didn't need to carry the heavy brick alone anymore. He could include others and lead people in a different way.

No wonder I hadn't found the right answer, Jack realized. *I was asking the wrong questions.*

"But where do I start and what steps do I take to get everyone involved in the tough decision?"

"You know who can help with that," his Dad replied as he sipped the last drop from his coffee cup.

Jack nodded. *It was time to visit Ron.*

Chapter 9

To Sift and Distinguish: Mission Discernment

Jack parked in the circular driveway leading to the three story brick home. He rang the doorbell, the door opened and Ronald Webster warmly greeted him.

"Thank you so much for seeing me on short notice," Jack said as he stepped through the doorway.

"My pleasure," Ron replied as he took Jack's overcoat. "I'll always make time to see one of my best students. It's been a joy following your growing career and family over the years."

Jack briefly considered sharing the news about Amy's pregnancy, but he followed his privacy instincts and said nothing.

Ron had achieved success by devoting his time and talent helping others. Along the way his career evolved with success in multiple industries across multiple decades.

Well known as a trusted resource to hospital leaders across the nation, Ron developed long personal and professional relationships which, as he said, "enriched me far more than I could possibly benefit anyone else."

More recently Ron was serving as a university faculty member for graduate capstone courses to medical students and healthcare administration students. He still had multiple business interests, but spent most of his time mentoring and teaching others.

Ron liked to share the most frequent question he was asked. "People ask if I consider myself a businessperson or a teacher," he said. "I answer yes."

Jack had been a student in Ron's capstone master's business decision making course. Today was the first time Jack had seen Ron face-to-face in several years, but it was like they had just spoken yesterday.

"When you called, you described a difficult decision your hospital is facing," Ron began as they settled at the table in his four season porch, each holding a cup of hot coffee.

"Yes," Jack answered. "The physician who does most of the deliveries at our small hospital has resigned, and there seems to be no way to replace him that is financially or logistically feasible. This affects the entire service and lots of people."

Ron nodded.

"I've been trying to find the answer myself," Jack said. "But the problem is much bigger than me."

"Right now opinions differ and emotions are running high," Jack said. "I'm here because I need to learn a new approach. I want to lead the process so the hospital and community make a difficult decision *together*."

Long pause.

"I think I know what I need, but I don't know how to get there," Jack said.

"What do you need?" Ron asked.

"I need other people to understand hospital realities. And I need other people to review the situation and help select the best choice for the future," Jack answered.

"Right now I'm stuck," Jack said. "I need a step-by-step guide to approach an important, difficult decision."

"Your instincts are right on," Ron said in his calm, soothing voice. "People will rally around an idea when they understand realities and where the leader is taking them."

"You're the master at this and I need your help," Jack said with a slight smile.

Ron sipped his coffee thoughtfully. Then he set the cup down gently.

"I'd be happy to help," he began. "It will be my pleasure to share five steps that will lead from conflict to community support and help your hospital and community discern an appropriate choice - especially when alternatives are limited."

"Thank you!" Jack said. "I knew you would take us where we need to go. We can start finding dates for you to come to town as soon as possible, we'll line up people for you to meet, places for you to gather with others, a nice apartment while you are in town, arrange meals, get you a car…"

Ron waited for Jack to finish.

"Not exactly what I had in mind," he said.

Jack tilted his head to one side.

"You need to show yourself that you are the right person to lead this journey, and I will be happy to teach you," Ron said.

"From there you'll lead the effort, not me," Ron continued. "I'll show you a path that you can share with the community so everyone knows *how* and *why* a decision was made."

"Jack, as you've seen, the obstetrics challenge you face goes to the heart of the organization and community. The Five Steps help your organization answer a key question: *who are we*? Once you know that, you are prepared to make a decision based on the fundamental mission and values the organization treasures."

"Along the way I suspect you'll also answer those same questions more clearly about yourself, too," he said.

Jack was ready for the challenge. "When can we start?" he asked.

Ding dong! The front doorbell rang.

Ron rose from his chair and went to answer the door.

"How about right now?" Ron asked as he walked down the hallway.

Jack reached into his bag to grab paper and a pen.

Jack could hear familiar greetings and upbeat conversation getting closer as Ron escorted the visitor back to the porch.

Jack recognized the visitor immediately as he rose from his chair. An energetic man in his late-forties with a wide, sincere smile, Karl Burnett was the state's most popular legislator. Karl was that rare public servant universally respected by voters, employees, lobbyists, other governors – name the group and Karl had earned their respect.

Recently Karl had done the seemingly impossible by assembling members from both major parties as a team to craft state marijuana legislation that satisfied the parties, the public, the business community, and legislative leaders.

The legislation had passed in truly bipartisan fashion and the state's leading newspaper ran a block headline: *Burnett Continues To Show What It Means to Lead.*

Before entering politics, Karl had built a successful career as an economic development director. During his economic development tenure, Karl brought together local businesses, education leaders, elected officials, students, retired people and anyone else who could help recruit a business to town. He had developed a reputation for constant attention to the mission and using creative methods to bring resources together to accomplish a goal.

"The first filter is always to review mission and values," Karl would tell Boards and business leaders. "Then we factor in other layers like budget and operational impact."

Karl's relentless focus on mission and values at every level had earned him the nickname "Mr. Mission Possible." There are worse names they could call me, he often said.

Of course Ron would know Karl Burnett, Jack thought, *and of course Karl is sitting with us right now.*

Ron introduced the two men and smiled broadly as Karl and Jack shook hands.

"Please, have a seat," Ron said as they all sat down. "We have much to discuss."

Karl didn't waste any time. "Ron tells me you have a major decision facing your hospital," he began.

"Yes," Jack said. "I hate to admit it, but I'm not really sure what to do next or how to do it."

"Let me say how much I appreciate your difficult situation and your candor," Karl began. "It sounds like you're ready to go a few layers deeper to enrich your decision-making."

Jack was all ears.

"Let me share some thoughts about mission discernment to add to what you already know," Karl began. "First let's discuss the meaning of mission discernment. I always like to remind people that discernment comes from the Latin root *discernere* – "to sift or distinguish.""

"So at its core, with mission discernment *we are trying to distinguish the appropriate path forward using multiple filters* in spite of obstacles and distractions."

"Life today is crazy busy. I know CEO's often spend their days providing fast-paced answers to everyone who approaches them with a need."

"Have you ever kept an activity log?" Karl asked, "My guess is that a rural hospital CEO provides at least 30 to 50 answers to someone about something every day. Maybe more."

"On the other hand, mission discernment," Karl continued, "is more reflective and requires added perspective and quiet time. *The focus is on questions as much as answers.* People define discernment concepts in different ways. Some think the whole idea is to recognize new choices. Others try to grasp what is obscure."

He paused. "However you choose to look at discernment, the key is to seek input and experience from others to sift through the choices to find a solution that may not satisfy everyone, yet aligns with your organization's mission and values."

"To be honest, getting all that input and working through others sounds like a lot of work," Jack replied. "I have been in my small hospital for quite a while so I think I know the operation pretty well."

Ron joined the conversation. "I'm sure you do, Jack. But let me add to the conversation by asking you a few questions."

"Please do," Jack replied.

"The last time you needed to see a local provider about some topic, did you make an appointment on their schedule and sit in the waiting room until the assigned time, or did you walk through a back hallway and catch the provider between patients for a brief conversation while other patients sat in the waiting room?"

Jack replied. "Ok, you got me. I stopped the physician in the clinic hallway and we talked while patients waited in the exam rooms."

Ron replied. "Remember, Jack, this isn't a gotcha moment but rather a reflection to add to your learning." Karl nodded in agreement.

"Another question for you, Jack," Ron continued. "When you or a family member needs to see a provider for your own health, do you call the main clinic scheduling number or do you get on the schedule some other way?"

Jack thought back to the past three times he had seen his own physician. Each time the clinic staff had simply added his appointment when he had a break in his meeting schedule.

"Got me again," he said. "Clinic scheduling staff just add me in when it works on my meeting calendar."

"And one more to emphasize the point," Ron said. "Jack, have you ever really worried about having the financial means to make a $10 copayment for a physician visit?"

Jack shook his head no.

"All of this simply reminds you that individuals experience the healthcare system in very different ways," Ron concluded. "As leaders *we need to look at more realities than our own*, so the extra work for extra perspective is worth it in the long run."

"I understand your point about mission and values," Jack said, "but it still seems like an obstetrics physician's resignation and replacement is a business decision that an administrator can analyze and then make a recommendation to the Board."

"I can see why you feel that way," Karl said. "But here's a way I think about the difference between a business decision and something deeper: I think a business decision can often be solved by some expert in the field, someone we contact like a consultant or an accountant. Our best action in that case is to work our contact list and find the right person who can solve the problem."

"But think of the topics that touch on the soul of the organization or the identity of the community," he said. "A *mission discernment process helps us go deeper, looking through multiple lenses*, to appreciate different perspectives for those deeper issues. With this approach, we include many people with many viewpoints."

"So I can just look at the mission and values and ignore the business side?" Jack said.

"That would be nice, wouldn't it?" Karl said, smiling broadly. "The whole idea is to address major administrative, operational or clinical issues in line with our organizational mission and values."

"So I consider mission and value discernment not *in lieu of* operational decision-making or strategic planning, but rather *an additional layer to add nuance and context* to tactical decision making," Karl added.

Jack sat back and collected his thoughts for a moment. "It seems like a fine line between making a business decision and applying a mission discernment process."

"There are nuances," Ron said. "Of course it is up to you and your Board whether the possible elimination of obstetrics deliveries in your rural community qualifies for a mission discernment." He knew Jack would need to embrace the concept himself to lead authentically.

"I see what you're saying," Jack said. "But this all sounds like a lot of work and my calendar is jam-packed already because I wear lots of hats in our small hospital."

"A mission discernment process invites others to help so you don't carry it alone," Karl said. "We acknowledge we can't do everything by ourselves and we invite people with different views and talents to make valuable contributions to the conversation."

"Now let's talk about creating a team that will help do some of the heavy lifting," Karl said.

He continued. "Ron asked me to reflect and prepare remarks and learnings from some recent mission-based processes I have facilitated," Karl said. "From my experience, effective teams need some specific competencies."

"Thank you for sharing," Jack said with pen in hand.

"My experience is that we need a team of people who can *help listen to community members* in large or small groups; someone who can *help review data*; people to *process different types of information*; people to *see beyond themselves to the bigger picture*; people willing to *speak respectfully and work with others;* people who can *review different alternatives,*" Karl rattled off ideas quickly. "We need people who can *work with others* and r*each consensus.*"

Karl paused. "Thoughts?"

"That makes perfect sense," Jack said. He wished he would have thought of those criteria himself.

Karl looked at Ron. "Do you want to tell him?"

"You're on a roll," Ron said. "Keep going."

"Jack, you know your local situation best. I offered some ideas, but you need to apply your own experience. Your task now is to generate a list of possible candidates who could be invited to participate on a core mission discernment team," Karl said.

"I'll give you some time to create your list, Jack," Ron interjected. "Tomorrow you'll learn how to prepare yourself and other key players for an inclusive discernment process. Then shortly after that we'll discuss your team ideas."

Jack nodded as he took notes.

"Karl, thank you," Jack said as all three men rose. "You've been amazing."

As he started to sense the possibilities, Jack went home that day wired, not tired.

Chapter 10

Step One: Prepare Yourself and Other Key Players

You Can't Blow an Uncertain Trumpet (Theodore Hessburgh)

Ron and Jack settled into comfortable chairs at a circular table in the lower level of Ron's home. A large movie screen hung from the opposite wall.

The table was equipped with a computer console. Jack noticed the green button was lit.

"As you have been experiencing," Ron said, "When an event happens and a CEO faces a major decision, it is critical to prepare yourself personally for the leadership challenge ahead. Why? First, the event, by definition, has caused a change from your own normal. You can't go about your regular day."

Tell me about it, Jack thought.

"Secondly, *your leadership attitude, behavior and tone will set the stage for the entire process.* The shadow you cast will impact everything."

Images were running through Jack's mind. *What example have I been setting?*

Ron turned his attention to the console. He typed a code number and the teleconference equipment came to life.

"I'm excited for you to meet Joan Keldon," he said. "While the teleconference connects, let me give you a brief background. Joan is administrator of a rural hospital that needed to decide whether to continue inpatient services. This was a big decision for the community, and people had different opinions. Joan's background as a psychologist was invaluable. She led the community through the Five Steps and today the hospital is growing and the community has a can-do spirit of new innovation. Her personal preparation was fantastic because she…"

Joan's smiling face appeared on the movie screen.

"Can you hear me?" Joan's voice came through the speakers.

"Perfectly," Ron answered. "Can you hear us?"

Joan nodded.

"Thanks so much for joining us, Joan," Ron said. "It will be helpful for us to hear your experience preparing for the crucial discussions your facility went through a while back."

Joan inhaled and exhaled slowly before she started.

"I heard what you are going through with OB deliveries, and it sounds familiar," she said to Jack. "For what it's worth, when we first learned we had a mission-critical decision ahead of us, I took some time having a talk with myself. *Before I could help our organization understand what it stood for, I needed to clarify what I stood for.* I wrote down my own values. Then I reflected on how those values translated to the situation."

"For example, I asked myself if a public conversation aligned with my own values, or did it feel like airing dirty laundry? I considered what personal consequences I would face by sharing every appropriate fact and educating like never before. How would this impact my career? What would my peers say? How would this look to others?"

Joan paused. "I'll admit I was feeling sorry for myself. I was anxious. I didn't feel courageous. But eventually that personal values reflection helped me see the situation as a chance to live my values for others to see." She paused. "I made notes in a journal which later gave me courage to work through some tough conversations."

Ron said, "I know you had plenty of stress. Why not just resign and find another role somewhere? Or simply let events unfold and see how things go?"

Joan laughed. "Believe me, I thought about it. I knew I had several choices. I could resign the position and look elsewhere; I could recognize there was a problem but focus on other things and be slow to respond; I could talk to a few insiders behind closed doors and "announce" some answer, or I could bring others into the conversation and let them help."

Ron and Jack nodded toward the screen.

"Then a very wise person said something that rang my bell," Joan winked into the camera.

"*You can't blow an uncertain trumpet*," she said. "I thought that was a classic Ron original, but he told me that Father Theordore Hesburgh gets credit for that phrase."

"Around then I realized that a difficult challenge was exactly why I had devoted my career to rural healthcare," Joan said. "I knew I needed to believe in myself, in the process, and I needed to move forward confidently with each step even when the outcome was uncertain."

Jack listened.

"But the truth was…" Joan paused. "The truth was, in the beginning I wasn't confident. The idea of closing the inpatient unit and talking openly to the community was outside my comfort level. I didn't know exactly what skills I would need, but I figured whatever those skills might be, I didn't have them."

"But now I can give you some idea of what to expect," Joan continued. "I learned that to lead this process with confidence, one way or another the CEO needs access to certain skills."

"I would love to hear specifics," Jack said. "That will help me know how prepared I'm going to be for the task at hand."

"It's wise to start thinking now, "Joan said. "And remember: even if these skills are not your strengths, you can ask for help from someone else to fill in the blanks. I know our tendency is to do everything ourselves. But my life became much better when I asked others to help."

"I'm taking copious notes," Jack said. "Would you describe the skills the situation called for, please?"

With a smile Joan held up her left hand to the camera and pointed to her five fingers with her right hand.

"I think those leading transparent mission conversations need access to five specific skills," she said. "First is the *ability to clearly communicate vision and values.*"

"Because mission discernment processes will discuss problems that go to the nature of "who we are" as an organization, leaders must be able to communicate a sense of purpose, talk about future possibilities, and create a long-term vision understood by everyone," she said.

"I tend to focus on just today or this week instead of the long-term," Jack admitted. "Keep going."

"Next, you will need to *exercise listening skills more than ever before,*" Joan continued. "What does this look like? Practice attentive and active listening. Be someone who has the patience to hear people out. Someone who can accurately restate the opinions of others, even when he or she disagrees."

"That last part can be hard," she added with a small grin. Jack wondered how well he would be able to deliver all of these skills.

"Third, this will be a period where you will need to gain perspective. Mission-critical problems require leaders who can look toward the broadest possible view of some challenge. This individual needs a strong future orientation to discuss "what if" scenarios with ease, and the ability to discuss different aspects of the same issue."

"I'll just keep rolling," Joan said with her hand to the camera. "Fourth is the ability to *deal with ambiguity*. Because a variety of unique solutions will be offered by different community stakeholders, discernment leaders must be able to shift gears comfortably and maintain composure when the picture is blurry."

"Keep rolling," Jack said as he listened and wrote notes.

"Lastly, you'll need *excellent presentation skills*," she said. "You'll be telling the story in a new way. Because you will be speaking to a wide variety of audiences in different settings, discernment process leaders must possess the skills to communicate one-on-one, in small groups, large groups, with community leaders, and the general public."

"So expertise in writing presentations and sharing stories is critical. My experience is that both data and stories are necessary parts of presentations to accurately tell the story," she said.

"Extremely helpful, Joan," Jack said. "I do worry a bit because I struggle with a few of those skills."

Ron spoke in his calming voice. "Here's your chance, Jack," he said. "Your chance to involve others to complement your own skills. Notice Joan said *the process* needs those skills, not necessarily one person. Remember you have others on your administrative team, other employees in the organization, Board members, medical staff members – literally anyone you know could be invited to lend their talents."

"Here's another benefit to reaching out for help," Joan added. "We opened our own eyes to the incredible talents of employees. One example we had here was a clinical employee who had remarkable artistic abilities. He could draw beautiful cartoons, caricatures, scenery, you name it. And shame on us. We were not aware of that talent because we had never asked."

"Later our artist clinician helped create very popular posters and other written communication during the discernment process," she added.

Ron said, "Imagine the talent in your organization if you look beyond job descriptions."

Jack nodded.

"Now let's talk about helping other key players prepare," Joan said. "Keep in mind that those around you have a stake in the process and ultimately will answer for your actions in addition to their own. Probably my best conversation with my Board Chair was early in the process where we had a heart-to-heart conversation," Joan trailed off for a moment, lost in the memory.

"During that conversation we were honest with each other about our fears and our hopes, and that helped us set expectations for each other," she continued. "For example, we agreed how frequently I would update her, and I promised to text her immediately if anything happened out of the norm."

"This was important to both of us," she said, "because she wanted to trust me to proceed and frankly, I didn't want her at the hospital every day crossing boundaries trying to be the CEO."

"That's why a visible plan with specific steps is so helpful," Joan continued. "Once you have that plan, you can share it with every interested person so people know what's going on."

"I imagine it was the same situation with your medical staff leader and senior team?" Jack asked.

"Exactly. Preparation began by understanding fears and concerns and then coming to an agreement about how and when we would communicate," Joan explained. "I'm happy to say that we emerged with a closer bond after this experience than we ever had before."

Jack nodded.

Joan looked off camera and gestured to some unseen person. She looked back into the camera. "Sorry, gentlemen, something unexpected needs my attention. But Jack, before I go, let me emphasize something you already know," she began. "*The key to preparing key players is to let them know what you expect to happen, and when.* And then set expectations about how and when you will communicate with each other."

"The whole idea is to avoid nasty surprises, obviously," she said. "That helps everyone move forward with confidence and energizes those who wish to follow."

"In other words, we blow a certain trumpet," Jack said enthusiastically.

"Absolutely!" Ron said, laughing. "Thank you so much for your time, Joan."

"Thank you, Joan," Jack added. "Can't tell you how much I appreciate your insight."

"Call if you need anything," Joan waved and disappeared from the screen.

Jack sat quietly.

"Ron, thank you," Jack said. "Everything seemed blurry before, but now things are becoming more clear."

"An important Step One, my friend," he answered. "There is much more to come."

Ron clicked off the teleconference console as Jack packed his papers.

"I'll see you in the morning to discuss Step Two," Ron said as Jack headed to the front door.

I wouldn't miss it for the world, Jack thought.

Chapter 11

Step Two: Recruit the Mission Discernment Team

What we need are more people who specialize in the impossible

(Theodore Roethke)

Ron was waiting outside the next morning when Jack drove up the driveway. Holding two travel mugs of coffee, Ron smiled as Jack approached.

Always ready to go, Jack thought to himself.

"Good morning," Ron said as he handed a mug to Jack and closed the car door.

"Thank you," Jack said as he drove down the driveway. "I can use the caffeine after a late night putting my core mission discernment team candidate list together."

Ron nodded and motioned with his hand. "Please turn right at the end of the driveway. They'll be waiting for us when we get there."

Jack nodded and turned out of the driveway. No destination just yet, so he simply drove straight down the tree-lined street.

"What's up for today?" Jack asked.

"New views. Fresh perspective. No preconceived notions," Ron answered. "The best way to spend a day."

Jack smiled and knew exactly where they would go.

Pulling into University parking Lot A, Ron handed Jack a faculty parking pass for the machine. The arm went up quickly and Jack pulled into an open space reserved with a sign that said *R. Webster, Faculty.*

Miller Hall was straight ahead. Jack felt the familiar rush of recognition and gratitude mixed with fond memories.

A life-changing building, he thought. *I met Ron here.*

Meanwhile, Ron had opened the passenger door and started to climb out of the car before Jack even shifted to park.

Fourteen students were already seated in a conference room when Jack and Ron arrived. The room grew quiet and wide grins broke out around the table. Ron gracefully made eye contact with every person in the room.

"Good morning!" Ron said enthusiastically.

"Good morning, Professor Webster!" came warm, energetic replies.

"Jack, our class is comprised of second year medical students and second year master's degree students in the hospital and health administration program," Ron announced. "Everyone, this is Jack McGee. I'm proud to call Jack my friend. He himself graduated from this program some years ago, and now he is the CEO of a small rural hospital."

Jack smiled. The students came from diverse backgrounds and geography, representing over eleven states and three countries. The class included students who had earned undergraduate degrees in nursing, public health, accounting, history, and even philosophy.

After a full year and a half together as a class cohort, the students enjoyed a healthy camaraderie.

"Jack is facing a major decision at the hospital," Ron continued. "I thought we would all benefit from an idea exchange."

"Your job during this seminar," Ron told the students, "is to listen, question Jack's rationale, and be ready to add new ideas."

"Take it away, Jack," Ron said. "What's the situation, and what are you thinking?"

Jack cleared his throat. "Thanks everyone. We had big news at our hospital recently which has knocked us for a loop. One of our local physicians, the one who delivers 98% of the babies, resigned a few weeks ago with 90 days notice. His departure puts the entire obstetrics service at risk. It's financially difficult if not impossible to recruit a replacement physician."

"One of the biggest issues is that the community's identity is about growth and entrepreneurship and exceeding small town expectations," Jack explained. "People consider local baby deliveries as a symbol of future community growth."

"I've come to realize that the topic is not just about staffing and the budget, but about who we are as a hospital and community," he said.

"After the physician's resignation, honestly, I tried to solve this problem myself. That went nowhere fast. With Ron's help I'm realizing we need more people and a new approach to address the situation."

"And selfishly," Jack added, "I don't want to shoulder the burden by myself anymore."

Several students nodded.

"To help make the best decision and build widespread community support, we want to invite a diverse group of people to join a core mission discernment team to help seek public input, review facts, and look for alternatives," Jack continued. "And then make a recommendation to our Medical Staff and Hospital Board of Trustees."

"Why will a team of people with vastly different viewpoints help make the best decision, Jack?" Ron asked.

"Because people have different experiences when it comes to healthcare," Jack replied. "Various viewpoints from engaged people will help generate additional alternatives."

"So basically you need people who are passionate about the hospital for some reason and like to argue their point," offered Mary, a clinical nurse manager in the master's program.

"That sounds like a nightmare," Brad, an undergraduate accounting major, said to the laughter of his fellow students. "It'll be time consuming and you'll need to listen to people who don't know what they're talking about."

"Exactly the point, Brad," Ron said. "That's why it's so important for the CEO to help people 'know what they're talking about'. People can't support a situation if they aren't aware a problem exists, so the CEO has to find a way to teach as many people as possible to see all the pieces of the puzzle."

Beth was currently completing an internship in the University hospital legal department. She raised her hand and Ron nodded to encourage her to speak.

"Here's what I don't get," Beth began. "Why hash all this out publicly before you even have a solution?" she asked. "Wouldn't it be better to keep this quiet while you study it? We learned in the Healthcare Law class that hospitals like yours can legally go into closed session for certain topics. You could avoid a lot of hassle and stress from people in the community asking you questions when you don't know the answers."

Jack nodded. "That's the way I'm leaning right now," he said. "First, most community residents won't want to be associated with this big problem, so a closed session committee process would help participants stay anonymous. I thought Merrill, our Board Chair, Dr. Molson, our Chief of Medical Staff and I could call some people and ask them to come and listen to what we are facing and give us different ideas to study the problem."

Jack continued, "During the process, the group could meet with the Board members in closed session as often as necessary to keep everyone up-to-speed, and then the recommendation itself could be at a closed Board meeting. This would allow facts to be shared and people to speak their minds freely. Then maybe the day after the Board makes a decision, we could schedule employee meetings and issue a press release to announce what we've decided to do."

Several students tilted their heads.

"That way we control the information and release it in a certain order according to our plan," Jack added.

More head tilts.

Ron just listened. His patience and silence made space for someone else to provide feedback.

After a brief pause, one student with a wide, toothy grin started shaking his head slowly back and forth.

Ron said, "Care to share your thoughts, Tim?"

"No, not really," Tim answered, flashing that wide smile again. Everyone laughed, including Ron and Jack. An undergraduate philosophy major, Tim was whip smart with blond, longish curly hair, a wide smile and generous personality. He had become a favorite among his classmates because he always made time to listen and offer an idea to help.

"No offense, and I don't want to start a big argument here," Tim continued. "But think about it: everything is instant communication and livestreamed these days. Do you really think you can control information and release it in a certain order, *especially* in a small town?"

Tim continued, "Besides, if this topic is that important to your community, why would everything be behind closed doors?" He leaned back and took a bite from a banana.

Ron could see the wheels turning in Jack's mind.

"But closed sessions are meant to discuss strategy," Jack said. "And discussing major service lines like obstetrics is certainly strategic."

Ron asked, "Tim, how would you reply to that view?"

Tim shrugged. "I guess it's about trade-offs. If you want more people in town to help make big decisions and support a decision, then you need to let go of some control and be completely transparent so they have the facts."

"Or," Tim added, "You can choose to use a smaller group to make the decision, but don't be surprised at the reaction when people find out."

"Outstanding insights, everyone," Ron said. "Jack. Tell us who you plan to invite to the core team, and reasons why."

Jack looked at his handwritten notes. Last night he had brainstormed ideas and shared them with Amy after she had put Charlie to bed. Amy didn't know the specific players, but as tired as she was, she was able to listen and ask "why that person?" now and then. Jack appreciated her loving gesture.

"We need two hospital decision makers, so two hospital Board members," he said.

Beth chimed in, "Please don't forget any open meetings laws that might apply."

"Will do," Jack replied. "We're fine because it takes five for a quorum."

He continued, "The Chair of our Medical Staff and at least one Medical Staff member who has a large infant and children clinic practice."

Ron prompted Jack, "Thoughts about other healthcare insiders?"

Jack looked at his list. "I'm thinking of our Laboratory Director and Director of Physician Services because those leaders see patient processes directly every day."

Tim raised his hand slightly. Ron nodded toward him.

"Who is the person in your facility who knows everyone and knows exactly what is going on at all times?" Tim asked.

Jack smiled. He was thinking of someone in the patient registration area.

"We have that person," Jack said. "But if she's in the group we might as well use a megaphone to shout everything to the world."

"I thought sharing appropriate information with others was the whole idea," Tim replied. "Assuming, of course, that you get some coaching from your hospital attorney about specifics."

Jack nodded. He added the patient registration employee to his list.

"You have a wonderful start, Jack," Ron said. "Now how about external community representatives?"

"Well, there is a retired nurse in town who is deeply respected," Jack answered. "She would speak her mind based on forty years of nursing perspective."

"Perfect," Ron replied.

"Another external community audience would be elected representatives, so I'm thinking of a City Council member and County Chancellor representative," Jack said.

He glanced back at his notes. "That would give us about ten members on the core team," he said.

Ron stood. "Thanks, Jack. Let's take a 20-minute break. Student colleagues, during the break, please gather in small groups and identify other core team candidates that Jack could consider. Select a spokesperson and be ready to present when we reconvene," he said.

As the break began, Jack was thankful for new ideas. But he couldn't shake the self-doubt. *Will an open public process make me look like the CEO who couldn't do the job?*

Ron sensed Jack's inner conflict. Before leaving the room, Ron leaned closely toward Jack's face and put his hand on Jack's shoulder.

"Courage," Ron said softly.

Jack nodded and slowly lifted his hand to give the thumbs up sign.

The class reconvened and everyone took their seats. Jack sat beside Ron, curious and ready.

"Who wants to go first?" Ron asked.

Mary spoke. "I'll go. We think the hospital needs to hear from people directly affected by the big decision. Jack, given that this is about obstetrics and local deliveries, we think you need to invite an expectant mother or two onto the core team. Even better would be someone who has been visible or vocal already."

Mary continued, "If you invite the most vocal critic expectant mother, you get access to a person who has already shown she is willing to devote her time, expertise and passion toward a topic. Why not educate that individual as best you can. Who knows? Maybe you *both* will learn something."

Heather Wyler, the woman who visited me that rainy night at the hospital? Jack wondered. *Imagine the two of us working together on this problem.*

Why not? he asked himself.

Mary looked around the room. "That's it for our group."

Liza motioned with her hand. "I'll report. We think a community healthcare professional like an optometrist, a dentist, someone from public health, a pharmacist, a chiropractor, or a long-term care facility employee should be included."

"Here's why," she continued. "Those professionals probably know the patient experience better than many hospital insiders because they refer patients to the facility and hear how things went."

"I drew the short straw and will go next," Tim said. "Buckle up for this one," he added.

"Because the goal of the process is to share information like never before in a way people will understand it, we think you should invite your local newspaper editor or radio station DJ or other media person to participate on the team."

Jack raised his eyebrow and leaned back in his chair.

Tim continued. "We get it. Most organizations treat the media like an outsider, like something that needs to be managed. But why not view your local media for what it is, which is an organization with trained individuals who make a living by sharing stories of local importance?"

Jack could just imagine the reaction of his Board members and hospital employees. Not to mention the hospital attorney.

"What if they report something they shouldn't and that gets us into trouble?" Jack asked.

"Does your team plan to do something that could get you into trouble?" Tim replied.

"No. Not intentionally, anyway," Jack said.

"Then what's the worry?" Tim asked.

Tim continued. "All we're saying is that your local media can be a powerful partner to help you get what you want, if you stop viewing them as the enemy."

"Besides, how powerful would that message be to the public that you are serious about transparency?" Tim said.

Ron nodded. "Thank you, Tim. Looks like we have one more group to report."

Darren began. "Here's what we talked about. Your goal is to focus on the long-term mission of the hospital. Most rural communities probably have had some form of local healthcare for seventy-five to one-hundred years. During that century, someone has fulfilled the mission to provide healthcare to local residents, even though the specific services have certainly changed over the last century."

When you put it that way, Jack thought, *the changes happening today are just one more example of the changes which have occurred over the past 100 years in our community.*

"We think this team needs the perspective of your local community librarian," Darren continued. "Librarians typically have strong organizational talents, research skills, appreciate historical storytelling, and interact with community patrons every day. We even brainstormed about finding a photo of the first house or facility from last century. Imagine using that photo in your community conversations today to remind people that progress required change and how far you've come."

Ron smiled and looked around the room. "Terrific thinking, everyone. Thank you so much for the privilege of participating in this conversation."

"Jack, you were writing notes during this discussion. Will you please summarize the representatives you believe would comprise an outstanding mission discernment core team?" Ron asked.

"Let's see," Jack said as he read his notes. "Two hospital board members. Two medical staff members. Two department leaders. An employee that serves as an informal opinion leader. A patient or two personally affected by the topic. A respected retired employee. A city and county elected representative. Two allied health professionals. The media editor. Our librarian."

Jack looked around the room. "Of course we can add or amend if we need another viewpoint, but this is a fantastic start. Thank you, everyone."

Ron announced, "That's it for today, everyone. Thank you for sharing your talents."

The students packed laptops, paper and pens into computer bags and backpacks and filed toward the door with comments like "glad we could help" and "best of luck."

Jack was quiet as he drove Ron home.

Pulling the car to the front door, Jack turned off the engine. Ron made no effort to open the passenger door.

"It really hit me when I wrote the final list of core team participant candidates," Jack said. "Every person on that list lives in our small town and wants what is best for the community. Every person would probably do anything to help, if asked."

"Agreed," Ron said. "My guess is that your invitation will get an instant yes."

Jack continued, "Honestly, I've been afraid of this topic and afraid of some of the people on that list. I can't even say exactly why."

"But today made sense to me," Jack said. "Our session showed how each person can contribute a piece to the bigger puzzle. Without the different perspectives, the puzzle would be incomplete."

"I just need to do the same thing," Jack concluded.

"*Now* we're getting somewhere!" Ron exclaimed with a fist pump.

Ron partially opened the passenger door and began to climb out.

"9:00 am tomorrow work for you?" Ron asked before closing the door.

"Count on me!" Jack said as he put the vehicle into gear.

Chapter 12

Step Three: Define the Major Issues and
Identify Stakeholders

Clarity is the moment we see without opening our eyes.

(Stephanie Banks)

Cynthia Zucker appeared on the video screen at 9:00 am.

"Good morning!" she said brightly.

"Good morning, Cynthia," Ron replied. Jack waved to the camera with a smile.

The two men were back at Ron's home, joining a video conference with a friend of Ron's well-versed in making difficult mission-based decisions for healthcare facilities.

Cynthia was a well-known and well-respected leader in the acute care rehabilitation industry. Originally a nurse by training, Cynthia had devoted her life to the growth, development and financial turnaround of rehabilitation facilities after her teenage son had suffered a devastating injury in a skiing accident. Serving as a caregiver to her paralyzed son for several years had given Cynthia a deep perspective into the patient experience and how acute care rehabilitation facilities can better meet needs.

These days Cynthia provided a referral-only advisory service and had helped dozens of acute care rehabilitation facilities navigate difficult decisions using mission, values and operating frameworks.

People she helped said they appreciated her philosophy and practical ideas to put concepts to work. As one CEO recently emailed to Cynthia: "The fact is, we can't just sit around talking about mission. We need actionable advice about processes so that decisions balance mission, values, and making payroll that week. You helped make that happen, so thank you."

"How is your son John doing these days?" Ron asked warmly.

"He's doing very well," Cynthia replied. "He lives independently in his own apartment, his job is going well and I'm pleased to say he's been dating a terrific young lady," she said with a smile. "We'll see where that goes. Dating is so different for young people today."

Ron laughed. "I can imagine. So glad to hear he's doing well."

"Ron, we'll always remember the tremendous kindness and support you showed after the accident," she said.

"My pleasure and privilege," Ron said. He took a breath. "Ok, we know you have many demands, Cynthia, so to respect your time, let me introduce you to Jack McGee."

Jack and Cynthia smiled to one another.

"How may I help you, Jack?" Cynthia asked.

"As Ron may have shared," Jack said, "A key physician has resigned at our hospital which puts the obstetrics service at risk. There seem to be so many things swirling around, I would appreciate your help listing the issues we should address so I can take that list to our core mission discernment team."

Ron smiled and looked at the screen, allowing Cynthia to reply.

Cynthia nodded. "Completely understand, Jack, and I can see why you have asked that question."

Cynthia looked into the camera. "Here's what I have found: *the best way to identify the major issue isn't to know the answers, it's to know the questions to ask.*"

She continued, "I know you are assembling a core team to provide additional ideas and your group probably hasn't worked together before, so one way to break the ice is to use a 3 X 5 white card method to get started."

"Will you explain that? I was wondering how to get the ideas flowing," Jack said.

"You might consider distributing a short stack of 3 X 5 white cards to each team participant at the beginning of the meeting. Give the group five minutes for each participant to write down a different issue on a separate 3 X 5 white card. Set a timer. At the end of the five minutes, ask each person to stack the cards in priority order."

"Normally I then ask for volunteers to recite the top five cards in their stack. This technique makes it easier for even the introverted team members to share their thoughts. And of course others compare their issues and their priorities along the way."

"Won't that highlight that everyone sees a different issue and has a different priority?" Jack asked.

"Exactly. This gets the discussion started, and then the leader can begin to pose questions for team conversation together. *Are there multiple issues at work here? What issues might be put in a 'parking lot' to review later? What are the issues for patients? What are the issues for the hospital? How about issues for the community? Are there common issues? Where issues are different, but maybe overlapping?*

Jack was listening and visualizing the meeting. No doubt there would be plenty of issues with so many diverse participants.

"You might consider asking a recorder to write the issues on a flipchart, Jack," Cynthia continued. "At a minimum, team members begin to see the complexity of the situation. It may not seem like it, but you are already building support because people appreciate the different viewpoints and the complexity."

Jack was glad to hear that. "I see where you're headed here, Cynthia," he said. "We create a brainstorming environment to surface the issues, and then we ultimately select the top four or five issues that need attention."

"Do either you or your hospital have the time and energy to deal with four or five major issues right now?" Cynthia inquired.

Pause.

"No," Jack answered.

Cynthia asked, "Then what needs to happen?"

Jack changed his thinking. "We need to filter issues down to the top issue and maybe a secondary issue."

"Exactly. Remember, if a team member feels strongly that some issue needs attention, you can always address it another way or another time."

"For now, *the core team needs focus and clarity to agree on the issue to address.* This helps everyone walk in the same direction and removes personal agendas early in the process."

"It takes some work, but your future self will thank you for spending time defining the primary issue now," Cynthia said. "Once you have defined the major issue, your team can begin to identify the key stakeholders to the topic."

Ron joined the conversation. "Cynthia, do you remember the situation in the western state when our local CEO skipped the stakeholder step?"

Cynthia smiled. "How could I forget? Jack, we had a situation where our company owned two separate rehabilitation facilities in the same large city. Financially, the downtown site was really struggling, so we needed to discern the right path given those challenges."

Ron was shaking his head at the memory.

Cynthia continued, "The local CEO reported to me at the time and I was aware he had embarked on a discernment process. For whatever reason, he became impatient. Once the core discernment team defined the issue, he moved directly to identifying options and solutions without identifying stakeholders and listening to those stakeholders."

"So an announcement was made that the downtown facility would close. Turns out that facility had a major financial benefactor with very strong feelings about the facility," Cynthia said. "I had to hold the phone about six inches from my ear the day the headline hit the newspaper and the donor called."

Ron nodded. "We're still trying to repair the trust in the relationship with him."

"So the lesson is to define the issue as clearly as possible so that you can identify stakeholders to consult with."

Cynthia asked, "Is it ok if we take a 10-minute biological break and then reconvene to discuss the next step?"

"Of course," Ron answered.

Cynthia stood and moved out of camera range to reveal a plaque hanging on her wall:

A thorn of experience is worth a wilderness of warning.

I'm blessed to be learning from those who have been there, Jack thought to himself as he headed for the restroom.

Ron and Jack were back around his conference table and Cynthia was at her desk.

"As we were discussing," Cynthia began. "After identifying the primary issue, the core team needs to identify the relevant stakeholders. We do this for at least two reasons. One, *identifying stakeholders helps us know who we must hear from. Second, we can clarify which stakeholder group will be making the final decision."*

Jack leaned forward. "That last point is critical, because the truth is that the Board of Trustees will make any final decisions. I don't want the core team to misunderstand that."

"Exactly why we have a step to discuss stakeholders and stakeholder roles," Cynthia said. "Jack, from your view, who might be stakeholders in your particular situation?"

"I was thinking about that as you spoke," Jack said. "For our obstetrics problem, certainly expecting mothers are a stakeholder. But so is a 90 year-old male or 45 year-old mom with teenagers if they lose access to care because of the problems with the obstetrics service."

He continued, "And what about the donor who financially supports the hospital? I also thought of local vendors who serve the hospital. Not to mention employees. All of those stakeholders might be affected. And that's just off the top of my head."

Jack paused. "I'm sure the core team will think of other stakeholders, too. I can see this really opening the eyes of people who are advocating only their own perspective."

"Here's my parting thought, Jack," Cynthia said. "Remember that every group has something to say. Embrace that."

"With that, I need to go, gentlemen," Cynthia said. "Call me anytime!" Ron stood and waved to the screen. "Until next time, my friend."

"Thank you!" Jack said with a wide smile.

Now that it was midafternoon, Ron waited for Jack to summarize the day's conversations.

"I feel like I am finally starting to connect the process to the stakeholders we serve," Jack said. "That's what you mean by 'deeper understanding', isn't it?"

Ron nodded. "All connected to the spirit of mission, not just practical, tactical daily problems."

"I'll admit that's the hard part for me," Jack confessed. "Making a connection to the mission can be tricky because there are so many daily demands otherwise."

"Sometimes understanding comes in very unlikely places, Jack," Ron said. *"Be open to learning anywhere and everywhere."*

A pause.

"Be here at the same time tomorrow morning?" Ron inquired.

"Plan on me!" Jack said as he lifted his bag to his shoulder. He was ready to leave because he had a scheduled oil change in a few minutes. He figured he should get there because he had canceled the last two appointments. His trusty Taurus was ready.

Chapter 13

An Oil Change that Changed Everything

Jack pulled into the painted lane of the auto service shop two minutes before his scheduled appointment. He handed the keys to an earnest young man in his early 20's holding a clipboard. The auto technician was a familiar face because the young man's father was a physical therapist at the hospital.

"Just the oil change today, Mr. McGee?" the technician asked.

"Please," Jack replied as he climbed out of the car and headed for the waiting room.

The lobby/waiting area only had one other customer at this late hour. A big-screen television played an afternoon syndicated talk show in the background amid the smell of brewed coffee.

Jack broke into a wide smile when he recognized Violet Marsh patiently waiting in one of the chairs.

"Violet!" Jack said as he approached with arm outstretched to shake her hand. "What a pleasure. Long time no see."

Violet broke into a wide grin as she shook his hand. "Jack! So nice to see you. Always makes my day."

Now in her mid-80s, Violet still lived independently in the Marsh family home and remained active in numerous women's groups and other causes in the community. Violet and her husband had raised six children. All six had moved to other states as adults but each held a steadfast commitment to returning home for the annual mid-July Marsh family reunion. The gathering drew the adult Marsh children, their large families and many extended cousins and other relatives. Barbeque, lawn games and raucous laughter were hallmarks of those gatherings at the Marsh family home. Most reunion weekends converted to a neighborhood block party because Violet led life with the "everyone is welcome, we'll set a plate for you" mentality.

Violet's husband Frederick had been a long-time family medicine physician in town. Dr. Fred Marsh had practiced full-time in that same community for nearly 50 years before retiring. When Fred had passed away five years ago, the funeral procession included, as most people said, "every person in this town and every township within 20 miles."

Jack took a seat near Violet. He had told Amy once that Violet Marsh reminded him of a down-to-earth Queen Elizabeth. With beautiful white hair, lines around her eyes and a wide smile, Violet's calm demeanor exuded the gentle manner of a woman who had seen everything. Jack felt comfortable around Violet; with her he was completely open and willing to show vulnerability.

"I'm so glad to run into you, Jack," Violet said. "I had been planning to stop by your office this week and now here you are!"

"I know how busy you must be, but there are a couple things I want to share with you and something I want to give to you," Violet added.

"Well, we've definitely had our hands full at work, that's for sure," Jack said.

Violet nodded. "How are you doing?" she asked. She was well aware of the contention at the hospital and in the community.

Jack said, "Much better after the past few days. I've been learning to look at the situation in a whole new way and I'm optimistic we'll find the best path forward."

Violet patted his hand. "I'm thrilled to hear that. I can understand why Dr. Smith wanted to stop delivering babies, but I also know the problem that creates for our hospital."

She continued, "Looking back, I can't tell you how many holidays and weekends Fred needed to leave on short notice to deliver a baby. Or wait to deliver a baby. Or wait and then the baby decided it's not time," she said with a laugh.

"Those were trying times and sometimes I would tell Fred how frustrating it was," Violet said. "He would always hold my hand and listen, and then he would say *We're on a mission together, Vi. We take care of patients. This isn't just what we do, it's who we are.*"

"As tired or frustrated or disappointed I was, Fred always recognized and appreciated my role at home and how that allowed him to see patients when they needed help," she said.

"Together we just decided we were a team and we would see this as our life's mission."

Fred and Violet lived their mission statement before it was vogue to put it on walls, Jack thought.

"Which was a good thing, by the way, because early on the money was pretty tight," Violet said. "Particularly when our kids were young and the farm economy struggled. Fred never pressed patients to pay when he knew they couldn't."

"I know people are upset right now about this possible obstetrics change," Violet continued. "But lately I've been thinking over the fifty years Fred practiced and all the changes he made. He added new things, updated some procedures or stopped doing certain procedures if it was better to be done somewhere else, that sort of thing."

Jack nodded. He glanced around, hoping no one would interrupt their conversation.

Violet said, "People forget how things have evolved for decades. And I know this current situation is important. But Fred had such a knack to look past the details of the day and go to the heart of the matter." Violet leaned over to pick up her purse from the floor beside her chair.

"I want to give you something that I have carried in my purse for a long time," she said as she flipped through the inside purse pockets.

"Oh heavens, Violet, I couldn't possibly accept anything..." Jack began to protest.

"Please, I want you to keep this as a reminder like Fred did for so many years," Violet said as she pulled out a piece of yellowed paper about 8 ½ inches long and 2 inches wide, folded in half. Jack could only make out a small handwritten date in pencil on the aged paper.

"Many years ago Fred and his partner were working long hours with no vacation as they constantly built new services at the clinic and hospital. All while seeing patients all day, every day and most evenings, too."

"Anyway, things at the clinic and hospital were changing fast and patients were upset, the town seemed upset, and even some of our friends were frosty for a while."

Violet's eyes grew moist and she sniffled back tears. "In that period, it was hard for me to watch the toll everything took on Fred. He worked long hours and still gave his best at home. Never once did he show doubt or frustration. I don't know how he did it, but he always, and I mean always, saw life through our mission."

Jack grabbed a tissue from a box on the table and handed it to Violet.

She dabbed her eyes and continued, "After Fred passed away, I was going through some things he had kept in his office desk. Mixed in with routine papers was this slip of paper that he had placed under the glass on his desk as a daily reminder."

Violet unfolded the paper. Fred had written across the paper in his distinctive cursive handwriting:

We'll change our <u>way,</u> but never our <u>why</u>.

"I thought you should have this, Jack," Violet said, placing the paper in his hand.

"Help people understand why, and the way gets easier," she said. "I promise."

Jack looked at the piece of paper in his hand. He imagined the challenges Dr. Marsh had seen over the years.

Jack felt energized.

By this time the service technician was walking toward the waiting area.

"Mrs. Marsh, your vehicle is ready," he said, handing her the keys. "Thank you so much for your patience with us. Would you like me to drive you home?"

"Of course not," Mrs. Marsh replied. "I can drive myself."

Jack rose and the two embraced in a hug.

"Thank you," he whispered in her ear.

"You got this, Jack," she whispered back.

Jack sat thinking of Dr. and Mrs. Marsh and the life they built together. His car was ready.

Now ***that's*** *connecting your life to a mission,* Jack thought.

He felt goosebumps as he climbed into his car.

Chapter 14

Step Four: Identify Alternatives and
Compare to Values

All truths are easy to understand once they are discovered;
the point is to discover them (Galileo Galilei)

Another day of discovery for Jack.

Jack keypunched digits while Ron introduced the plan for the morning.

"We have been gifted a complimentary online pass to a meeting of Hospice leaders from across the country," Ron explained. "My dear friend Frances Harrington, a longtime Hospice advocate and administrative leader is the keynote speaker."

Jack finished typing and pressed the Enter button. The system began to process remote access.

"Hospice programs throughout America have been battered by reimbursement challenges, staffing challenges and about every other challenge you can imagine," Ron continued. "Frances has been instrumental in guiding mission-based conversations in dozens of organizations as new choices were considered."

The movie screen filled with the image of a national meeting stage, complete with large logos and professional lighting.

"Looks like we logged in at the perfect time," Jack said.

"Must be nearly 1,000 people in that room," Ron guessed.

Announcer voice: "Ladies and gentlemen, here to describe highlights from a career making decisions to advance the Hospice model, Frances Harrington!"

Frances walked onstage with a beaming smile and strode to the podium amid loud applause.

"What are we to do?" Frances began with a confident tone as her eyes scanned the large, darkened auditorium. "How are we to decide the best course of action when there are so many choices?"

Pause for effect.

"What is the *right thing* to do in these uncertain times?" she exclaimed.

Colorful photos of various Hospice patients and staff members from different organizations scrolled on a large screen behind Frances as she spoke, making her remarks more personal for everyone.

"Those are tough questions, and I don't really have the answers," she said. "But I know my mom had great advice."

"Tell us!" someone said loudly from the first few rows. The audience laughed.

Frances shielded her eyes from the lights and looked in that direction. "I'm getting there," she said with a wide smile.

"My mom told me: *be adventurous in life, but don't stray too far from the well.*"

Another pause.

"Our values are 'the well,' my friends," Frances said softly. "*What we value becomes our point of contact reminding us who we are and what we stand for.*"

"Quite a speaker and quite a message," Jack said. Ron nodded.

Frances continued. "So here's what we do: We *know* our programs need to change with the environment. We *know* we can explore new models to serve our clientele. And we *know* there will be uncertainty that can only be addressed by experimentation."

"The key to staying true to ourselves and our Hospice values will be the questions that we ask. We need to *explore together whether a choice supports our values or works against our values.*"

"What are your organizational values? Here's our chance to discuss values with your teams and put words around them to deepen understanding."

Frances looked around the room. "Let me give you an example. Is one of your organizational values collaboration? Maybe that means you achieve more by working with others than you would alone. That clarity helps you assess future choices. Then we can reflect on key questions, such as whether the proposed alternative supports collaboration or works against it? Or how might the proposed change relate to other values?"

"We can work together to identify the values that define us and then consider how the proposed choice impacts that value."

"How am I doing so far?" Frances asked the audience of fellow Hospice leaders. A loud burst of applause.

"Then let me share another example: respect is a value of our Hospice movement. Maybe that means you respect the dignity of every human being. Now say you are assessing some alternative Hospice service model. Does the proposed alternative support the value? Are we respecting diverse opinions? And will we respect ourselves for the decisions made?"

"Consider the value, consider the impact."

Frances held up her pencil. "Of course another value is stewardship, which is the pledge to be stewards of resources far into the future. Do we have sufficient resources? If we dedicate resources to one effort, what service might be constrained? How will resource trade-offs impact the clients?"

"Consider the value, consider the impact," she repeated.

"Now maybe I'm making this sound easy, because it's not," Frances continued. "But *imagine the strength and stability we feel when we anchor our decisions to the solid foundation of mission and values.* This solid base creates a calm refuge for our reflection, even when the world is swirling around us."

Frances stepped back from the podium microphone to loud applause, providing a brief break in her comments.

Ron turned down the speaker volume and asked Jack, "What's running through your mind?"

Jack looked at Ron. "What a simple yet effective approach to assessing possible alternatives against our values. And I love the idea of a solid foundation in a swirling world. I know I could use that stability. Honestly, I'm excited to assemble the core team and get started with these discussions."

Ron nodded. "You've come a long way, Jack. Just a short while ago I doubt you could have said you're excited about any of this."

Jack answered, "That's an understatement if I've ever heard one!"

Chapter 15

Step Five: Make a Decision

Organizations are not a product of circumstances, organizations are a product of decisions (Stephen Covey)

Ron turned off the projector. He had been waiting for this opportunity for some time.

"As you know, Jack, eventually a decision must be made," Ron said. "As you've seen during this learning journey, completing each step prepares you and the core team members, and ultimately the Board to make a decision when the time comes."

Jack nodded. He was looking forward to leading the process so others could be aware of all the issues and help make a decision.

"Following the steps in order creates momentum for the outcome," Ron said. "By then the process should have provided sufficient information so core team members and others can support the way the process worked and the way the decision was made, even if it wasn't their personal preference."

"As usual, the way to deeper learning is to ask questions," Ron continued. *Do you feel satisfied with the decision, or do you feel something else? Can all participants on the core team support the decision? If not, have leaders discussed how to reconcile differences? What follow-up might occur after the decision?"*

"With a transparent process and the steps we have learned, the organization and community will have the best chance to make a decision consistent with the mission and values of the organization," Ron said.

"You've taught me so much, Ron," Jack said. "I can never repay you."

"No need, my friend," Ron said. "Just go be you and unleash the power of the community working together to do the rest."

Chapter 16

The Journey Begins

Around 200 people sat around circular tables in the hospital cafeteria. The hospital had promoted an open informational meeting for anyone interested to learn more about the situation facing obstetrical services. Jack had solicited input from the board, medical staff and senior team members to plan the evening as a way to share information and describe the Five Steps of mission discernment.

Young mothers held toddlers and infants, elderly women sat together, obstetrics department nurses all occupied a table and dozens of other hospital employees sat with various family members. Two hospital board members sat at a table with a local media representative ready with a recording device, paper and pencil. A City Council member, County Chancellor and a large partner health system representative completed that particular table.

Tension was in the air. The topic was important and opinions differed. Emotions ran high as Jack stood at the front of the cafeteria surrounded by a laptop, projector and high-tech microphone and speaker system. Ron always emphasized how important it was to use a high quality sound system for large public forums. "People came to learn. And they can't learn if they can't hear the presenter," he said.

"Which is your favorite TV doctor?" Jack's voice came through the speakers loudly and clearly. An image of several famous TV doctors was projected onto a large screen on the wall. The evening had begun.

"The goal tonight is to share information about the obstetrics service, and then describe where we go from here."

"In other words, let's all learn the same information so we can begin facing the same direction," Jack continued. "At least as much as possible at this stage in the journey."

For weeks Jack had dreaded having a public conversation about the problem. He had lost sleep and worried about the reaction. He had wondered how he could ever lead a productive meeting in these circumstances.

Yet tonight Jack felt calm inside. The people and the stories Ron had brought into Jack's life had helped build courage, one step at a time. Whereas before Jack dreaded the idea of a public gathering, tonight he relished the opportunity to share the hospital's reality.

"My team and I will answer any questions you have tonight," he said. "As openly and clearly as we possibly can."

Jack advanced to slide one and read it aloud, "*True or false: A critical access hospital gets cost based reimbursement, which means every penny of expense gets reimbursed by the federal government.* Please grab a pen and paper at your table and write down your answer."

Jack paused, and then offered the answer: "That's false. Basic business rules still apply because only about 45% of costs are subject to cost-based reimbursement."

"In other words, just like any organization, the hospital needs to bring in more money than it spends in expenses."

Slide two. Question: *How many patients does our local hospital and clinic serve every week? A. 100; B. 250; C. 500; D. 1,000.*

Jack waited for people to respond. Nearly every person was writing on their piece of paper.

"The answer is D, 1,000," Jack said. "We serve more than 1,000 people per week."

Jack moved to the next slide: *What does it cost per day to hire a fill-in obstetrics physician to be available to deliver babies? A. $100; B. $500; C. $3,000; D. $1,000.*

"The answer is C, $3,000 per day," Jack said. "That is just for the obstetrics doctor, which means the hospital must deliver enough babies to cover program expenses, or else the money must come from somewhere else."

Audience members leaned over to visit quietly with tablemates and share reactions. "I did not know that" and "I had no idea" was heard from around the room.

Jack could sense the mood in the room shifting from tension to curiosity.

Every piece of information Jack wanted to share was on a powerpoint slide, and every slide was in the form of a true/false, multiple choice, fill-in-the-blank or some other active question to engage the audience. This method allowed everyone to explore and discover learning themselves rather than just sit passively through one-way communication.

Next Jack posed a fill-in-the-blank question: *how much money does the hospital lose on the obstetrics service to deliver babies each year?* He then asked people to write their guess on a piece of paper.

"Let's have a few people read their guesses out loud." Jack began to call on random people. "Your guess, please? $5,000 loss? Sorry, that's incorrect. You, ma'am? $500 loss? Sorry, that's way too low. How about you, sir? $50,000? Heading the right direction, but way, way low."

People continued to guess from around the room. Finally one man says loudly, "$100,000 loss?" Jack made direct eye contact.

"Higher, sir," Jack said. "We haven't met yet. May I ask your name please?"

"Henry."

"Please keep going, Henry. A $100,000 loss is too low."

"$250,000 loss?" Henry replied.

"Still too low," Jack answered.

"$500,000 loss?" Henry ventured.

"Nope, keep going." A gasp across the room.

"A $1,000,000 loss?" Henry offered his last guess.

"Yep. That's right, just over a million dollar loss per year," Jack replied.

"*Are you shitting me*?" Henry exclaimed. People in the room laughed and Jack smiled. Henry's face turned red and he looked around.

"Sorry about that," he said. "Not in front of the kids."

"It happens," Jack said. "Besides, I feel the exact same way." Soft laughter in the room.

Ron's words echoed through Jack's mind. *Help people know what they are talking about. People can't support a situation if they aren't even aware a problem exists.*

After a few more slides, Jack shifted the conversation.

"So we have a problem." Heads nodded in agreement.

Jack continued, "Let me say that tonight we have no specific answers and no bombshell announcements."

Heads nodding again, appreciatively.

"What we do have is a specific process we will walk through so that we can understand the problem and craft an appropriate path forward."

"Let's talk first about who will be helping us tackle this problem. Because our goal is to get input from many perspectives, I'm thrilled to say fourteen people from the hospital and the community have committed to serving on a core team to work through a decision-making process."

Jack advanced to the next slide with the list of fourteen mission discernment core team members who would serve on the core team. He had already met 1:1 with each person to answer questions and discuss each of the Five Steps. All had agreed. Most were in the room that evening.

Hospital Board members (2)

Medical Staff representatives (2)

Hospital department leaders (2)

Hospital employee representative (2)

Retired former hospital nurse employee (1)

City Council member (1)

County Chancellor (1)

Woman using obstetrics services now (1)

Local Newspaper/Media editor (1)

Librarian (1)

People nodded in agreement as audience members read the list. Several leaned over to tablemates expressing surprise at certain names on the list. Jack heard "gutsy" and "wow" from audience members.

"Many, many thanks to these people for volunteering for this journey. I really appreciated our one on one conversations and am excited to work with everyone," Jack said. "Of course we may seek input from other people as needed along the way."

He continued, "What will this core team do? This group of volunteers will formulate a recommendation to the Medical Staff and ultimately to the hospital board of trustees."

"How? The core team will conduct a mission discernment process."

Jack paused.

"To tell you the truth, I only recently learned about this word "discernment." It comes from Latin, and means "to sift or distinguish." So we're going to take steps to sift through different choices about the obstetrics service. The core team will review this problem with regard to the business challenge and make sure future alternatives are consistent with long term hospital mission and values."

Jack advanced another slide. "Just so everyone knows, these are the Five Steps the core team will complete over the next few weeks."

Step 1: Prepare Administrative, Board and Medical Staff Leaders

Step 2: Recruit the Core Mission Discernment Team

Step 3: Define the Major Issues and Identify Stakeholders

Step 4: Identify Alternatives and Compare to Values

Step 5: Make a Decision and Recommendation to Hospital Board of Trustees

"We'll set ground rules at the first meeting, and please know we'll share as much information as possible with anyone who will listen," he said.

Several smiles around the room.

"Please look for regular updates over the coming weeks either from core team members, our local media partners, or from the hospital social media platforms," Jack said.

"Just like tonight, we want people to experience the same information, knowing we have different perspectives as we look for a path forward."

"Now, let's discuss some logistics and then we'll call it a night," Jack continued.

A few minutes later the meeting was over. Jack stood near the front of the room scanning the scene. People were talking. People were pointing at papers on the table and several people were writing notes. He saw heads nod and some people leaned forward energetically as they spoke. Members of the proposed discernment core committee were each surrounded by three or four other people who thanked them for participating and offered ideas about what could be discussed later in the upcoming core team meetings.

Jack walked quietly over to a round table with five people visiting. They glanced up and smiled and continued talking among themselves, not concerned that he was listening. "I had no idea..." one woman said to another. One woman addressed Jack. "Tell me one more time. Did I hear $3,000 per day to hire a fill-in doctor?" one young mother asked. Jack nodded. She shook her head.

Jack slowly walked back toward the front of the room and began unplugging the microphone and computer cords. He took a slow, deep breath and exhaled. The last piece of the large brick was finally off his shoulders.

As Jack slowly wrapped the cords together to put in the bag, he noticed Heather Wyler trying to catch his eye from across the room amid the crowd noise. The same Heather who had been ill-informed and had visited his office late one stormy night to announce a petition and community movement to block any changes at the hospital.

Heather smiled and flashed a "thumbs up" sign.

Jack nodded and smiled back.

Chapter 17

One Year Later: Giggling Babies and
Bright Balloons

Jack opened the community room door and smiled at the scene. Sunshine streamed through the windows and the room was buzzing with an energetic air of celebration. White tablecloths adorned with fresh flowers, colored balloons, festive napkins and decorated paper plates created a party-like atmosphere. A table with flavored punch, coffee and pastries lined the wall as upbeat music thumped from portable speakers to jam a happy background soundtrack for the occasion.

Around the room twelve to fifteen new mothers bounced healthy, giggling babies on their laps or stood rocking back and forth as they talked excitedly amongst themselves about daily schedules, family events and how quickly the days go. Jack's wife Amy held their daughter Lucy in her arms and waved with a wide smile when he entered the room.

Several providers, nurses and obstetrics employees were relaxed and smiling as they sat with patients they knew as friends and neighbors, enjoying the time together.

Violet Marsh, the woman who had shared the handwritten momento from her husband, Dr. Fred Marsh, was seated among the young mothers, enjoying every minute. Violet was so supportive of growing families that the young mothers made sure she was a part of this special celebration.

Jack made eye contact with Violet. He mouthed the words "thank you." She nodded her head slowly with a wide smile.

"Thank you for stopping by!" Linda, the obstetrics nurse program coordinator, said to Jack. "We have punch, pastries and coffee if you would like to help yourself."

"Thanks for having me," Jack replied. "I wouldn't miss this party for the world." Jack made eye contact with several providers and nurse employees and young mothers and smiled as he took a seat beside Amy and Lucy.

This day was a long time coming. It was fun to all sit together and visit with the new mothers and employees who had worked so hard to make it happen.

A short while later Linda turned the music down and good-naturedly tapped her plastic punch cup with a spoon. "Can I have your attention, please? All of us involved in the new obstetrics Sharing is Caring program just want to say a heartfelt thank you for your confidence in using the new service. The patient satisfaction surveys rate this service in the 98th percentile nationally. To our team at the hospital, your support today and those results mean the world to us."

She continued, "Now Dr. Rivers would like to say a few words."

A highly-respected, long-time local family medicine physician, Dr. Rivers rose from his seat and scanned his eyes across the room. "I have known many of you forever," he started. "Heck, I delivered some of you, and now you are mothers yourselves. I can't tell you how good that feels."

People in the room nodded and smiled.

"And how old that makes me feel," he added to laughter. "But back to the topic at hand," he continued with a smile. "We know it was a big change to stop delivering babies in this facility and that it was hard on everyone. Thank you for your courage to stick with us. We really think this program is the best way to care for you and your babies and we are all proud to be a part of it."

Applause from everyone in the room.

Standing and slowly rocking her baby boy, one woman shared with the group, "I think I speak for most of us here when I say this," she began. "We may have been nervous about the change at first, but we appreciate the care we received before the delivery, the delivery itself went just fine, and it is great being able to bring our babies back to the clinic in our own town."

Dr. Rivers said, "No doubt much has changed in the years I have been practicing and this is just another example."

"Linda, what's next?" Dr. Rivers said. "It's time for me to get another doughnut!" as he walked toward the pastry table.

Linda took the lead. "Now we'll have a drawing for a basket of bath oils…"

Jack had given Amy's hand a squeeze and kissed Lucy on the forehead before he quietly slipped out the door.

Walking to his office through the busy lobby area, he marveled at the difference from one year ago. So, so different.

It seems like yesterday and it seems like 10 years ago, he thought to himself.

Jack arrived at the door to the administrative office area and turned the handle to enter. The hydraulic hinge made the door silently open and close slowly.

As Jack waited for the door to fully open, he glanced back into the open lobby area. An extremely popular physician, Dr. Michael Pierce, was walking directly toward Jack with a sense of urgency.

In addition to serving as the inpatient unit medical director, Dr. Pierce was the number one admitting physician and was alone responsible for 95% of all inpatient admissions. His practice served complex patients and his philosophy was to utilize all ancillary services available at the facility.

In other words, a large percentage of patient care services and hospital revenue depended on Dr. Pierce.

Jack smiled and waved as he paused for the physician to approach.

Dr. Pierce didn't smile back and he was holding a white sealed envelope.

The End

Five Step Discernment
from Conflict to Community Support

Step One: Prepare Yourself and Other Key Leaders

Step Two: Recruit the Core Mission Discernment Team

Step Three: Define the Major Issues and Identify Stakeholders

Step Four: Identify Alternatives and Compare to Values

Step Five: Make a Decision or Recommendation

Visit my LinkedIn profile for more:
https://www.linkedin.com/in/doug-morse-mba-ma-b86a5088/

Acknowledgements

I would like to recognize the many volunteer Board of Trustee leaders, Medical Staff members, community leaders and healthcare colleagues I have worked with over the years. Living and working together in service to a common cause has been a tremendously rewarding privilege.

Certainly I am not the first to describe the principles of mission discernment. During my career, I found the following sources to be particularly helpful for insight and deeper understanding into challenging, mission-critical decision making: Covenant Health, Alberta, Canada; Catholic Health Initiatives, Englewood, Colorado and articles by Dr. C. Joe Arun, Director and Dr. Renu Isidore, Research Associate, Loyola Institute of Business Administration, Chennai, Tamil Nadu, India.

Special thanks to colleagues, family members and other supporters who invested time and energy reading early drafts of this work. Ann Morse, Aaron Morse, Claire Champlain, Abby Morse, Tony Cristoforo, Andrew Morse, Lauren Dettmer, Sheryl Fitzpatrick, Robb Gardner, Dennis Lee, Joseph LeValley, Paul Manternach, MD, Willis Scharmer, Bill Schickel, Candi Schickel, and Terry Schumaker were especially helpful. Thank you.

For templates to use during your own Five Step mission discernment process to lead from conflict to community support,

please direct message me on LinkedIn at
https://www.linkedin.com/in/doug-morse-mba-ma-b86a5088/

I am a rural healthcare zealot. My passion is supporting rural hospitals and physician clinics because I believe those facilities are the economic and healthcare engine of our rural way of life.

If you need a speaker, coach, strategist, advisor, or simply an ear to bend about rural healthcare issues, contact me at doug.morse@exechq.com or 480-447-2204.

You got this.

About the Author

Doug Morse, MBA, MA is a former rural hospital CEO and community college faculty member. A graduate of Luther College and the University of Iowa, today he helps C-suites and Board members build skills to innovate and make tough decisions the right way. During his career he was recognized with the "Young Executive Achievement Award" by the Iowa Hospital Association and he was twice recognized with the "Excellence in Education" award for his work as a full-time college business entrepreneurship instructor. He and his wife, Ann, are the parents of three adult children.

Special Thanks

Paul Manternach, M.D. is the Senior Vice President, Physician Integration/Chief Medical Officer at MercyOne North Iowa Medical Center in Mason City, Iowa. Board certified in Emergency Medicine and Family Medicine, he is a graduate of Grinnell College and the University of Iowa College of Medicine. Paul served as Chief Resident during his post graduate Residency, and was nominated "Teacher of the Year" seven times by the MercyOne North Iowa Medical Center Family Medicine Residency program. Paul and his wife, Jill, are the parents of four children.

Bill Schickel is serving his fifth term as Mayor of Mason City, Iowa. He previously served three terms in the Iowa House of Representatives where he chaired the Local Government Committee, Ethics Committee and Economic Development Appropriations Subcommittee. A retired broadcast executive, Bill and his wife, Candi, a Mason City attorney, are the parents of three adult daughters.